CW00407361

THIS BOOK BELONGS TO:

_____

_____

INDEX

INDEX

WINE Tasting

NAME	
VARIETAL	VINTAGE
PRODUCER	ALCOHOL %
REGION	PRICE
TASTED AT	DATE

👁 APPEARANCE

Color Hue
- ☐ Clear
- ☐ Straw
- ☐ Gold
- ☐ Brown
- ☐ Pink
- ☐ Salmon
- ☐ Orange
- ☐ Brick
- ☐ Ruby
- ☐ Garnet
- ☐ Purple
- ☐

Color Depth
- ☐ Pale
- ☐ Medium
- ☐ Deep

Clarity
- ☐ Clear
- ☐ Hazy
- ☐ Opaque

Viscosity
- ☐ Watery
- ☐ Medium
- ☐ Syrupy

AROMA

☐ Low ☐ Medium ☐ High Intensity

_____
_____
_____
_____
_____
_____
_____

TASTE

- ☐ Sweet
- ☐ Medium
- ☐ Dry
- ☐ Tart
- ☐ Fresh
- ☐ Flabby
- ☐ Light
- ☐ Medium
- ☐ Full-Bodied

_____
_____
_____
_____
_____
_____
_____
_____
_____
_____

FINISH

☐ Short ☐ Medium ☐ Long

_____
_____
_____

😋 FLAVOR WHEEL

Leather   Mushroom
Mineral   Woody
Earthy   Herbal
Honey   Spicy
Dark Fruit   Floral
Tropical Fruit   Grassy
Smoky   Coffee
Nutty   Chocolate

💬 ADDITIONAL NOTES

_____
_____
_____
_____
_____
_____
_____
_____
_____
_____

🍷 PAIRED WITH

☆ SCORE

/5☆

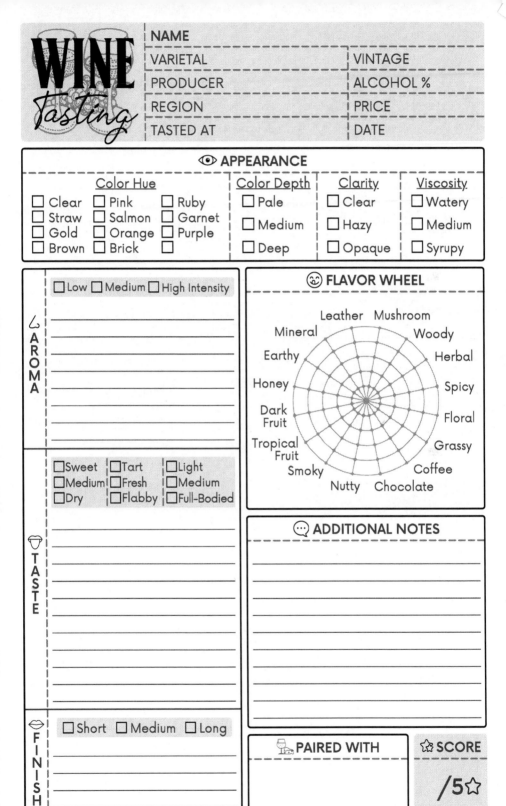

1

WINE Tasting

NAME	
VARIETAL	VINTAGE
PRODUCER	ALCOHOL %
REGION	PRICE
TASTED AT	DATE

👁 APPEARANCE

Color Hue
- ☐ Clear
- ☐ Straw
- ☐ Gold
- ☐ Brown
- ☐ Pink
- ☐ Salmon
- ☐ Orange
- ☐ Brick
- ☐ Ruby
- ☐ Garnet
- ☐ Purple

Color Depth
- ☐ Pale
- ☐ Medium
- ☐ Deep

Clarity
- ☐ Clear
- ☐ Hazy
- ☐ Opaque

Viscosity
- ☐ Watery
- ☐ Medium
- ☐ Syrupy

AROMA

☐ Low ☐ Medium ☐ High Intensity

_____
_____
_____
_____
_____
_____
_____

TASTE

- ☐ Sweet
- ☐ Medium
- ☐ Dry
- ☐ Tart
- ☐ Fresh
- ☐ Flabby
- ☐ Light
- ☐ Medium
- ☐ Full-Bodied

_____
_____
_____
_____
_____
_____
_____
_____
_____

FINISH

☐ Short ☐ Medium ☐ Long

_____
_____
_____

😋 FLAVOR WHEEL

Leather Mushroom
Mineral Woody
Earthy Herbal
Honey Spicy
Dark Fruit Floral
Tropical Fruit Grassy
Smoky Coffee
Nutty Chocolate

💬 ADDITIONAL NOTES

_____
_____
_____
_____
_____
_____
_____
_____
_____
_____
_____
_____

🍷 PAIRED WITH

☆ SCORE

/5☆

WINE Tasting

NAME	
VARIETAL	VINTAGE
PRODUCER	ALCOHOL %
REGION	PRICE
TASTED AT	DATE

👁 APPEARANCE

Color Hue
- ☐ Clear
- ☐ Straw
- ☐ Gold
- ☐ Brown
- ☐ Pink
- ☐ Salmon
- ☐ Orange
- ☐ Brick
- ☐ Ruby
- ☐ Garnet
- ☐ Purple
- ☐

Color Depth
- ☐ Pale
- ☐ Medium
- ☐ Deep

Clarity
- ☐ Clear
- ☐ Hazy
- ☐ Opaque

Viscosity
- ☐ Watery
- ☐ Medium
- ☐ Syrupy

AROMA

☐ Low ☐ Medium ☐ High Intensity

_____
_____
_____
_____
_____
_____
_____

😊 FLAVOR WHEEL

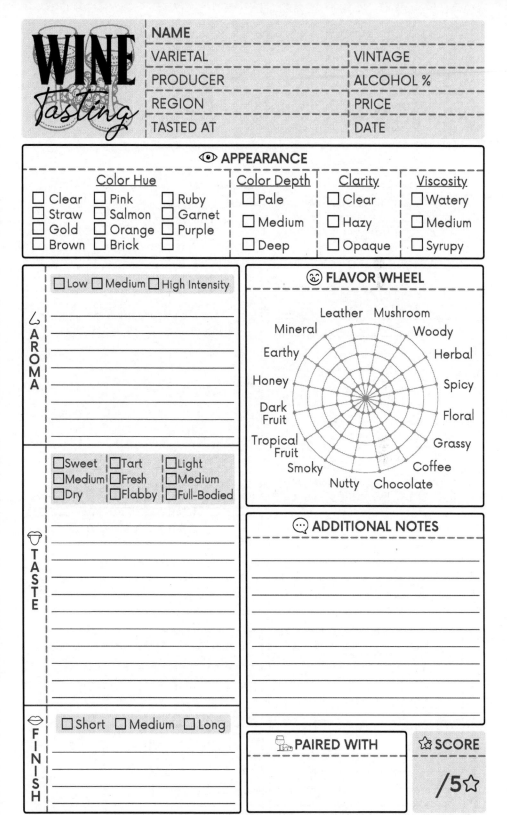

Leather Mushroom
Mineral Woody
Earthy Herbal
Honey Spicy
Dark Fruit Floral
Tropical Fruit Grassy
Smoky Coffee
Nutty Chocolate

TASTE

- ☐ Sweet
- ☐ Medium
- ☐ Dry
- ☐ Tart
- ☐ Fresh
- ☐ Flabby
- ☐ Light
- ☐ Medium
- ☐ Full-Bodied

_____
_____
_____
_____
_____
_____
_____
_____
_____
_____

💬 ADDITIONAL NOTES

_____
_____
_____
_____
_____
_____
_____
_____
_____
_____
_____

FINISH

☐ Short ☐ Medium ☐ Long

_____
_____
_____
_____

🍷 PAIRED WITH

⭐ SCORE

/5⭐

WINE Tasting

NAME	
VARIETAL	VINTAGE
PRODUCER	ALCOHOL %
REGION	PRICE
TASTED AT	DATE

👁 APPEARANCE

Color Hue
- ☐ Clear
- ☐ Straw
- ☐ Gold
- ☐ Brown
- ☐ Pink
- ☐ Salmon
- ☐ Orange
- ☐ Brick
- ☐ Ruby
- ☐ Garnet
- ☐ Purple
- ☐

Color Depth
- ☐ Pale
- ☐ Medium
- ☐ Deep

Clarity
- ☐ Clear
- ☐ Hazy
- ☐ Opaque

Viscosity
- ☐ Watery
- ☐ Medium
- ☐ Syrupy

AROMA
☐ Low ☐ Medium ☐ High Intensity

_____
_____
_____
_____
_____
_____
_____

TASTE
- ☐ Sweet
- ☐ Medium
- ☐ Dry
- ☐ Tart
- ☐ Fresh
- ☐ Flabby
- ☐ Light
- ☐ Medium
- ☐ Full-Bodied

_____
_____
_____
_____
_____
_____
_____
_____
_____

FINISH
☐ Short ☐ Medium ☐ Long

_____
_____
_____

😊 FLAVOR WHEEL

Leather Mushroom
Mineral Woody
Earthy Herbal
Honey Spicy
Dark Fruit Floral
Tropical Fruit Grassy
Smoky Coffee
Nutty Chocolate

💬 ADDITIONAL NOTES

_____
_____
_____
_____
_____
_____
_____
_____
_____
_____
_____
_____

🍷 PAIRED WITH

☆ SCORE

/5☆

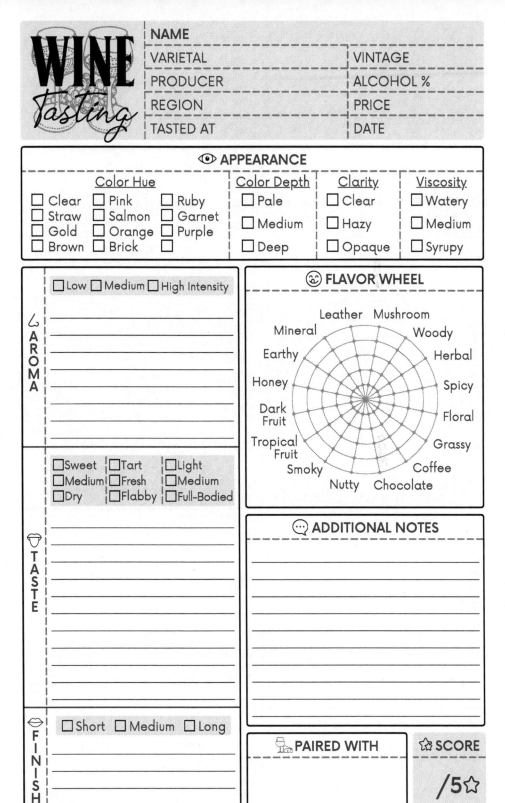

WINE Tasting

NAME	
VARIETAL	VINTAGE
PRODUCER	ALCOHOL %
REGION	PRICE
TASTED AT	DATE

👁 APPEARANCE

Color Hue
- ☐ Clear
- ☐ Straw
- ☐ Gold
- ☐ Brown
- ☐ Pink
- ☐ Salmon
- ☐ Orange
- ☐ Brick
- ☐ Ruby
- ☐ Garnet
- ☐ Purple

Color Depth
- ☐ Pale
- ☐ Medium
- ☐ Deep

Clarity
- ☐ Clear
- ☐ Hazy
- ☐ Opaque

Viscosity
- ☐ Watery
- ☐ Medium
- ☐ Syrupy

AROMA

☐ Low ☐ Medium ☐ High Intensity

_____
_____
_____
_____
_____
_____
_____

TASTE

- ☐ Sweet
- ☐ Medium
- ☐ Dry
- ☐ Tart
- ☐ Fresh
- ☐ Flabby
- ☐ Light
- ☐ Medium
- ☐ Full-Bodied

_____
_____
_____
_____
_____
_____
_____
_____
_____

FINISH

☐ Short ☐ Medium ☐ Long

_____
_____

😋 FLAVOR WHEEL

Leather Mushroom
Mineral Woody
Earthy Herbal
Honey Spicy
Dark Fruit Floral
Tropical Fruit Grassy
Smoky Coffee
Nutty Chocolate

💬 ADDITIONAL NOTES

_____
_____
_____
_____
_____
_____
_____
_____
_____
_____
_____

🍷 PAIRED WITH

☆ SCORE

/5☆

WINE Tasting

NAME	
VARIETAL	VINTAGE
PRODUCER	ALCOHOL %
REGION	PRICE
TASTED AT	DATE

👁 APPEARANCE

Color Hue
- ☐ Clear
- ☐ Straw
- ☐ Gold
- ☐ Brown
- ☐ Pink
- ☐ Salmon
- ☐ Orange
- ☐ Brick
- ☐ Ruby
- ☐ Garnet
- ☐ Purple

Color Depth
- ☐ Pale
- ☐ Medium
- ☐ Deep

Clarity
- ☐ Clear
- ☐ Hazy
- ☐ Opaque

Viscosity
- ☐ Watery
- ☐ Medium
- ☐ Syrupy

AROMA
☐ Low ☐ Medium ☐ High Intensity

_____
_____
_____
_____
_____
_____
_____

TASTE
- ☐ Sweet
- ☐ Medium
- ☐ Dry
- ☐ Tart
- ☐ Fresh
- ☐ Flabby
- ☐ Light
- ☐ Medium
- ☐ Full-Bodied

_____
_____
_____
_____
_____
_____
_____
_____
_____

FINISH
☐ Short ☐ Medium ☐ Long

_____
_____
_____

😋 FLAVOR WHEEL

Leather Mushroom
Mineral Woody
Earthy Herbal
Honey Spicy
Dark Fruit Floral
Tropical Fruit Grassy
Smoky Coffee
Nutty Chocolate

💬 ADDITIONAL NOTES

_____
_____
_____
_____
_____
_____
_____
_____
_____
_____
_____

🍷 PAIRED WITH

☆ SCORE

/5☆

6

WINE Tasting

NAME	
VARIETAL	VINTAGE
PRODUCER	ALCOHOL %
REGION	PRICE
TASTED AT	DATE

👁 APPEARANCE

Color Hue			Color Depth	Clarity	Viscosity
☐ Clear	☐ Pink	☐ Ruby	☐ Pale	☐ Clear	☐ Watery
☐ Straw	☐ Salmon	☐ Garnet	☐ Medium	☐ Hazy	☐ Medium
☐ Gold	☐ Orange	☐ Purple	☐ Deep	☐ Opaque	☐ Syrupy
☐ Brown	☐ Brick	☐			

AROMA
☐ Low ☐ Medium ☐ High Intensity

_____
_____
_____
_____
_____
_____
_____

😋 FLAVOR WHEEL

Leather   Mushroom
Mineral   Woody
Earthy   Herbal
Honey   Spicy
Dark Fruit   Floral
Tropical Fruit   Grassy
Smoky   Coffee
Nutty   Chocolate

TASTE
☐ Sweet ☐ Tart ☐ Light
☐ Medium ☐ Fresh ☐ Medium
☐ Dry ☐ Flabby ☐ Full-Bodied

_____
_____
_____
_____
_____
_____
_____
_____
_____

💬 ADDITIONAL NOTES

_____
_____
_____
_____
_____
_____
_____
_____
_____

FINISH
☐ Short ☐ Medium ☐ Long

_____
_____
_____
_____

🍷 PAIRED WITH

☆ SCORE

/5 ☆

WINE Tasting

NAME	
VARIETAL	VINTAGE
PRODUCER	ALCOHOL %
REGION	PRICE
TASTED AT	DATE

👁 APPEARANCE

Color Hue
- ☐ Clear
- ☐ Straw
- ☐ Gold
- ☐ Brown
- ☐ Pink
- ☐ Salmon
- ☐ Orange
- ☐ Brick
- ☐ Ruby
- ☐ Garnet
- ☐ Purple

Color Depth
- ☐ Pale
- ☐ Medium
- ☐ Deep

Clarity
- ☐ Clear
- ☐ Hazy
- ☐ Opaque

Viscosity
- ☐ Watery
- ☐ Medium
- ☐ Syrupy

AROMA

☐ Low ☐ Medium ☐ High Intensity

_____
_____
_____
_____
_____
_____
_____

TASTE

- ☐ Sweet
- ☐ Medium
- ☐ Dry
- ☐ Tart
- ☐ Fresh
- ☐ Flabby
- ☐ Light
- ☐ Medium
- ☐ Full-Bodied

_____
_____
_____
_____
_____
_____
_____
_____
_____

FINISH

☐ Short ☐ Medium ☐ Long

_____
_____
_____
_____

😋 FLAVOR WHEEL

Leather Mushroom
Mineral Woody
Earthy Herbal
Honey Spicy
Dark Fruit Floral
Tropical Fruit Grassy
Smoky Coffee
Nutty Chocolate

💬 ADDITIONAL NOTES

_____
_____
_____
_____
_____
_____
_____
_____
_____
_____
_____
_____
_____

🍷 PAIRED WITH

☆ SCORE

/5 ☆

WINE Tasting

NAME	
VARIETAL	VINTAGE
PRODUCER	ALCOHOL %
REGION	PRICE
TASTED AT	DATE

👁 APPEARANCE

Color Hue
- ☐ Clear
- ☐ Straw
- ☐ Gold
- ☐ Brown
- ☐ Pink
- ☐ Salmon
- ☐ Orange
- ☐ Brick
- ☐ Ruby
- ☐ Garnet
- ☐ Purple

Color Depth
- ☐ Pale
- ☐ Medium
- ☐ Deep

Clarity
- ☐ Clear
- ☐ Hazy
- ☐ Opaque

Viscosity
- ☐ Watery
- ☐ Medium
- ☐ Syrupy

AROMA

☐ Low ☐ Medium ☐ High Intensity

_____
_____
_____
_____
_____
_____
_____

TASTE

- ☐ Sweet
- ☐ Medium
- ☐ Dry
- ☐ Tart
- ☐ Fresh
- ☐ Flabby
- ☐ Light
- ☐ Medium
- ☐ Full-Bodied

_____
_____
_____
_____
_____
_____
_____
_____
_____
_____

FINISH

☐ Short ☐ Medium ☐ Long

_____
_____
_____

😊 FLAVOR WHEEL

Leather Mushroom
Mineral Woody
Earthy Herbal
Honey Spicy
Dark Fruit Floral
Tropical Fruit Grassy
Smoky Coffee
Nutty Chocolate

💬 ADDITIONAL NOTES

_____
_____
_____
_____
_____
_____
_____
_____
_____
_____
_____
_____

🍷 PAIRED WITH

☆ SCORE

/5☆

9

WINE Tasting

NAME	
VARIETAL	VINTAGE
PRODUCER	ALCOHOL %
REGION	PRICE
TASTED AT	DATE

👁 APPEARANCE

Color Hue			Color Depth	Clarity	Viscosity
☐ Clear	☐ Pink	☐ Ruby	☐ Pale	☐ Clear	☐ Watery
☐ Straw	☐ Salmon	☐ Garnet	☐ Medium	☐ Hazy	☐ Medium
☐ Gold	☐ Orange	☐ Purple	☐ Deep	☐ Opaque	☐ Syrupy
☐ Brown	☐ Brick	☐			

AROMA

☐ Low ☐ Medium ☐ High Intensity

_____
_____
_____
_____
_____
_____
_____

TASTE

☐ Sweet	☐ Tart	☐ Light
☐ Medium	☐ Fresh	☐ Medium
☐ Dry	☐ Flabby	☐ Full-Bodied

_____
_____
_____
_____
_____
_____
_____
_____
_____
_____
_____

FINISH

☐ Short ☐ Medium ☐ Long

_____
_____
_____

😋 FLAVOR WHEEL

Leather   Mushroom
Mineral   Woody
Earthy   Herbal
Honey   Spicy
Dark Fruit   Floral
Tropical Fruit   Grassy
Smoky   Coffee
Nutty   Chocolate

💬 ADDITIONAL NOTES

_____
_____
_____
_____
_____
_____
_____
_____
_____
_____
_____
_____

🍷 PAIRED WITH

☆ SCORE

/5 ☆

WINE Tasting

NAME	
VARIETAL	VINTAGE
PRODUCER	ALCOHOL %
REGION	PRICE
TASTED AT	DATE

👁 APPEARANCE

Color Hue
- ☐ Clear
- ☐ Straw
- ☐ Gold
- ☐ Brown
- ☐ Pink
- ☐ Salmon
- ☐ Orange
- ☐ Brick
- ☐ Ruby
- ☐ Garnet
- ☐ Purple
- ☐

Color Depth
- ☐ Pale
- ☐ Medium
- ☐ Deep

Clarity
- ☐ Clear
- ☐ Hazy
- ☐ Opaque

Viscosity
- ☐ Watery
- ☐ Medium
- ☐ Syrupy

AROMA
☐ Low ☐ Medium ☐ High Intensity

_____
_____
_____
_____
_____
_____
_____

TASTE
- ☐ Sweet
- ☐ Medium
- ☐ Dry
- ☐ Tart
- ☐ Fresh
- ☐ Flabby
- ☐ Light
- ☐ Medium
- ☐ Full-Bodied

_____
_____
_____
_____
_____
_____
_____
_____
_____
_____

FINISH
☐ Short ☐ Medium ☐ Long

_____
_____
_____

😋 FLAVOR WHEEL

Leather Mushroom
Mineral Woody
Earthy Herbal
Honey Spicy
Dark Fruit Floral
Tropical Fruit Grassy
Smoky Coffee
Nutty Chocolate

💬 ADDITIONAL NOTES

_____
_____
_____
_____
_____
_____
_____
_____
_____
_____
_____

🍷 PAIRED WITH

☆ SCORE

/5 ☆

WINE Tasting

NAME	
VARIETAL	VINTAGE
PRODUCER	ALCOHOL %
REGION	PRICE
TASTED AT	DATE

👁 APPEARANCE

Color Hue
- ☐ Clear
- ☐ Straw
- ☐ Gold
- ☐ Brown
- ☐ Pink
- ☐ Salmon
- ☐ Orange
- ☐ Brick
- ☐ Ruby
- ☐ Garnet
- ☐ Purple

Color Depth
- ☐ Pale
- ☐ Medium
- ☐ Deep

Clarity
- ☐ Clear
- ☐ Hazy
- ☐ Opaque

Viscosity
- ☐ Watery
- ☐ Medium
- ☐ Syrupy

AROMA
☐ Low ☐ Medium ☐ High Intensity

_____
_____
_____
_____
_____
_____
_____

TASTE
- ☐ Sweet
- ☐ Medium
- ☐ Dry
- ☐ Tart
- ☐ Fresh
- ☐ Flabby
- ☐ Light
- ☐ Medium
- ☐ Full-Bodied

_____
_____
_____
_____
_____
_____
_____
_____
_____
_____

FINISH
☐ Short ☐ Medium ☐ Long

_____
_____
_____

😋 FLAVOR WHEEL

Leather Mushroom
Mineral Woody
Earthy Herbal
Honey Spicy
Dark Fruit Floral
Tropical Fruit Grassy
Smoky Coffee
Nutty Chocolate

💬 ADDITIONAL NOTES

_____
_____
_____
_____
_____
_____
_____
_____
_____
_____
_____

🍷 PAIRED WITH

⭐ SCORE

/5☆

WINE *Tasting*

NAME	
VARIETAL	VINTAGE
PRODUCER	ALCOHOL %
REGION	PRICE
TASTED AT	DATE

👁 APPEARANCE

Color Hue			Color Depth	Clarity	Viscosity
☐ Clear	☐ Pink	☐ Ruby	☐ Pale	☐ Clear	☐ Watery
☐ Straw	☐ Salmon	☐ Garnet	☐ Medium	☐ Hazy	☐ Medium
☐ Gold	☐ Orange	☐ Purple	☐ Deep	☐ Opaque	☐ Syrupy
☐ Brown	☐ Brick	☐			

AROMA

☐ Low ☐ Medium ☐ High Intensity

_____
_____
_____
_____
_____
_____
_____

TASTE

☐ Sweet	☐ Tart	☐ Light
☐ Medium	☐ Fresh	☐ Medium
☐ Dry	☐ Flabby	☐ Full-Bodied

_____
_____
_____
_____
_____
_____
_____
_____

FINISH

☐ Short ☐ Medium ☐ Long

_____
_____
_____

😋 FLAVOR WHEEL

Leather   Mushroom
Mineral   Woody
Earthy   Herbal
Honey   Spicy
Dark
Fruit   Floral
Tropical
Fruit   Grassy
Smoky   Coffee
Nutty   Chocolate

💬 ADDITIONAL NOTES

🍷 PAIRED WITH

☆ SCORE

/5 ☆

13

WINE Tasting

NAME	
VARIETAL	VINTAGE
PRODUCER	ALCOHOL %
REGION	PRICE
TASTED AT	DATE

👁 APPEARANCE

Color Hue
- ☐ Clear
- ☐ Straw
- ☐ Gold
- ☐ Brown
- ☐ Pink
- ☐ Salmon
- ☐ Orange
- ☐ Brick
- ☐ Ruby
- ☐ Garnet
- ☐ Purple
- ☐

Color Depth
- ☐ Pale
- ☐ Medium
- ☐ Deep

Clarity
- ☐ Clear
- ☐ Hazy
- ☐ Opaque

Viscosity
- ☐ Watery
- ☐ Medium
- ☐ Syrupy

AROMA

☐ Low ☐ Medium ☐ High Intensity

_____
_____
_____
_____
_____
_____
_____

TASTE

- ☐ Sweet
- ☐ Medium
- ☐ Dry
- ☐ Tart
- ☐ Fresh
- ☐ Flabby
- ☐ Light
- ☐ Medium
- ☐ Full-Bodied

_____
_____
_____
_____
_____
_____
_____
_____
_____

FINISH

☐ Short ☐ Medium ☐ Long

_____
_____
_____

😊 FLAVOR WHEEL

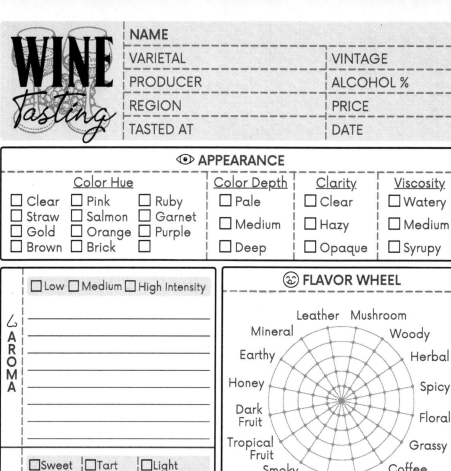

Leather   Mushroom
Mineral   Woody
Earthy   Herbal
Honey   Spicy
Dark Fruit   Floral
Tropical Fruit   Grassy
Smoky   Coffee
Nutty   Chocolate

💬 ADDITIONAL NOTES

_____
_____
_____
_____
_____
_____
_____
_____
_____
_____
_____

🍷 PAIRED WITH

☆ SCORE

/5 ☆

14

WINE Tasting

NAME	
VARIETAL	VINTAGE
PRODUCER	ALCOHOL %
REGION	PRICE
TASTED AT	DATE

◉ APPEARANCE

Color Hue
- ☐ Clear
- ☐ Straw
- ☐ Gold
- ☐ Brown
- ☐ Pink
- ☐ Salmon
- ☐ Orange
- ☐ Brick
- ☐ Ruby
- ☐ Garnet
- ☐ Purple
- ☐

Color Depth
- ☐ Pale
- ☐ Medium
- ☐ Deep

Clarity
- ☐ Clear
- ☐ Hazy
- ☐ Opaque

Viscosity
- ☐ Watery
- ☐ Medium
- ☐ Syrupy

AROMA

☐ Low ☐ Medium ☐ High Intensity

_____
_____
_____
_____
_____
_____
_____

TASTE

- ☐ Sweet
- ☐ Medium
- ☐ Dry
- ☐ Tart
- ☐ Fresh
- ☐ Flabby
- ☐ Light
- ☐ Medium
- ☐ Full-Bodied

_____
_____
_____
_____
_____
_____
_____
_____
_____
_____

FINISH

☐ Short ☐ Medium ☐ Long

_____
_____
_____
_____

☺ FLAVOR WHEEL

Leather   Mushroom
Mineral   Woody
Earthy   Herbal
Honey   Spicy
Dark Fruit   Floral
Tropical Fruit   Grassy
Smoky   Coffee
Nutty   Chocolate

💬 ADDITIONAL NOTES

_____
_____
_____
_____
_____
_____
_____
_____
_____
_____

🍷 PAIRED WITH

☆ SCORE

/5 ☆

WINE Tasting

NAME	
VARIETAL	VINTAGE
PRODUCER	ALCOHOL %
REGION	PRICE
TASTED AT	DATE

👁 APPEARANCE

Color Hue
- ☐ Clear
- ☐ Straw
- ☐ Gold
- ☐ Brown
- ☐ Pink
- ☐ Salmon
- ☐ Orange
- ☐ Brick
- ☐ Ruby
- ☐ Garnet
- ☐ Purple
- ☐

Color Depth
- ☐ Pale
- ☐ Medium
- ☐ Deep

Clarity
- ☐ Clear
- ☐ Hazy
- ☐ Opaque

Viscosity
- ☐ Watery
- ☐ Medium
- ☐ Syrupy

AROMA
☐ Low ☐ Medium ☐ High Intensity

_____
_____
_____
_____
_____
_____

TASTE
- ☐ Sweet
- ☐ Medium
- ☐ Dry
- ☐ Tart
- ☐ Fresh
- ☐ Flabby
- ☐ Light
- ☐ Medium
- ☐ Full-Bodied

_____
_____
_____
_____
_____
_____
_____
_____
_____

FINISH
☐ Short ☐ Medium ☐ Long

_____
_____
_____

😋 FLAVOR WHEEL

Leather Mushroom
Mineral Woody
Earthy Herbal
Honey Spicy
Dark Fruit Floral
Tropical Fruit Grassy
Smoky Coffee
Nutty Chocolate

💬 ADDITIONAL NOTES

_____
_____
_____
_____
_____
_____
_____
_____
_____
_____
_____
_____

🍴 PAIRED WITH

☆ SCORE

/5 ☆

WINE Tasting

NAME	
VARIETAL	VINTAGE
PRODUCER	ALCOHOL %
REGION	PRICE
TASTED AT	DATE

👁 APPEARANCE

Color Hue			Color Depth	Clarity	Viscosity
☐ Clear	☐ Pink	☐ Ruby	☐ Pale	☐ Clear	☐ Watery
☐ Straw	☐ Salmon	☐ Garnet	☐ Medium	☐ Hazy	☐ Medium
☐ Gold	☐ Orange	☐ Purple			
☐ Brown	☐ Brick	☐	☐ Deep	☐ Opaque	☐ Syrupy

AROMA

☐ Low ☐ Medium ☐ High Intensity

_____
_____
_____
_____
_____
_____
_____
_____

☺ FLAVOR WHEEL

Leather   Mushroom
Mineral   Woody
Earthy   Herbal
Honey   Spicy
Dark
Fruit   Floral
Tropical
Fruit   Grassy
Smoky
                      Coffee
Nutty   Chocolate

TASTE

☐ Sweet ☐ Tart ☐ Light
☐ Medium ☐ Fresh ☐ Medium
☐ Dry ☐ Flabby ☐ Full-Bodied

_____
_____
_____
_____
_____
_____
_____
_____
_____
_____

💬 ADDITIONAL NOTES

_____
_____
_____
_____
_____
_____
_____
_____
_____
_____
_____
_____

FINISH

☐ Short ☐ Medium ☐ Long

_____
_____
_____

🍷 PAIRED WITH

☆ SCORE

/5 ☆

WINE Tasting

NAME	
VARIETAL	VINTAGE
PRODUCER	ALCOHOL %
REGION	PRICE
TASTED AT	DATE

👁 APPEARANCE

Color Hue
- ☐ Clear
- ☐ Straw
- ☐ Gold
- ☐ Brown
- ☐ Pink
- ☐ Salmon
- ☐ Orange
- ☐ Brick
- ☐ Ruby
- ☐ Garnet
- ☐ Purple

Color Depth
- ☐ Pale
- ☐ Medium
- ☐ Deep

Clarity
- ☐ Clear
- ☐ Hazy
- ☐ Opaque

Viscosity
- ☐ Watery
- ☐ Medium
- ☐ Syrupy

AROMA
☐ Low ☐ Medium ☐ High Intensity

_____
_____
_____
_____
_____
_____
_____
_____

☺ FLAVOR WHEEL

Leather Mushroom
Mineral Woody
Earthy Herbal
Honey Spicy
Dark Fruit Floral
Tropical Fruit Grassy
Smoky Coffee
Nutty Chocolate

TASTE
- ☐ Sweet
- ☐ Medium
- ☐ Dry
- ☐ Tart
- ☐ Fresh
- ☐ Flabby
- ☐ Light
- ☐ Medium
- ☐ Full-Bodied

_____
_____
_____
_____
_____
_____
_____
_____
_____

💬 ADDITIONAL NOTES

_____
_____
_____
_____
_____
_____
_____
_____
_____
_____
_____

FINISH
☐ Short ☐ Medium ☐ Long

_____
_____
_____

🍷 PAIRED WITH

☆ SCORE

/5 ☆

WINE Tasting

NAME	
VARIETAL	VINTAGE
PRODUCER	ALCOHOL %
REGION	PRICE
TASTED AT	DATE

👁 APPEARANCE

Color Hue
- ☐ Clear
- ☐ Straw
- ☐ Gold
- ☐ Brown
- ☐ Pink
- ☐ Salmon
- ☐ Orange
- ☐ Brick
- ☐ Ruby
- ☐ Garnet
- ☐ Purple
- ☐

Color Depth
- ☐ Pale
- ☐ Medium
- ☐ Deep

Clarity
- ☐ Clear
- ☐ Hazy
- ☐ Opaque

Viscosity
- ☐ Watery
- ☐ Medium
- ☐ Syrupy

AROMA

☐ Low ☐ Medium ☐ High Intensity

_____
_____
_____
_____
_____
_____

TASTE

- ☐ Sweet
- ☐ Medium
- ☐ Dry
- ☐ Tart
- ☐ Fresh
- ☐ Flabby
- ☐ Light
- ☐ Medium
- ☐ Full-Bodied

_____
_____
_____
_____
_____
_____
_____
_____

FINISH

☐ Short ☐ Medium ☐ Long

_____
_____
_____
_____

😊 FLAVOR WHEEL

Leather Mushroom
Mineral Woody
Earthy Herbal
Honey Spicy
Dark Fruit Floral
Tropical Fruit Grassy
Smoky Coffee
Nutty Chocolate

💬 ADDITIONAL NOTES

_____
_____
_____
_____
_____
_____
_____
_____
_____
_____

🍷 PAIRED WITH

☆ SCORE

/5☆

WINE *Tasting*

NAME	
VARIETAL	VINTAGE
PRODUCER	ALCOHOL %
REGION	PRICE
TASTED AT	DATE

👁 APPEARANCE

Color Hue			Color Depth	Clarity	Viscosity
☐ Clear	☐ Pink	☐ Ruby	☐ Pale	☐ Clear	☐ Watery
☐ Straw	☐ Salmon	☐ Garnet	☐ Medium	☐ Hazy	☐ Medium
☐ Gold	☐ Orange	☐ Purple	☐ Deep	☐ Opaque	☐ Syrupy
☐ Brown	☐ Brick	☐			

AROMA

☐ Low ☐ Medium ☐ High Intensity

_____
_____
_____
_____
_____
_____
_____
_____

TASTE

☐ Sweet ☐ Tart ☐ Light
☐ Medium ☐ Fresh ☐ Medium
☐ Dry ☐ Flabby ☐ Full-Bodied

_____
_____
_____
_____
_____
_____
_____
_____
_____

FINISH

☐ Short ☐ Medium ☐ Long

_____
_____
_____

☺ FLAVOR WHEEL

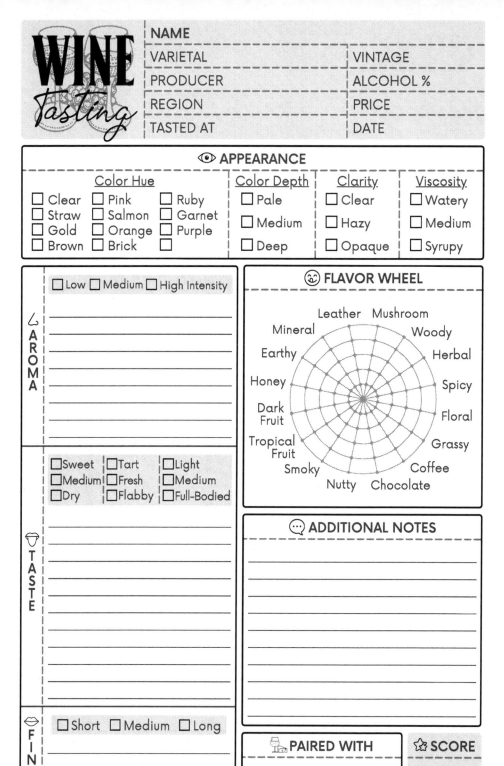

Leather Mushroom
Mineral Woody
Earthy Herbal
Honey Spicy
Dark Fruit Floral
Tropical Fruit Grassy
Smoky Coffee
Nutty Chocolate

💬 ADDITIONAL NOTES

_____
_____
_____
_____
_____
_____
_____
_____
_____
_____
_____

🍷 PAIRED WITH

☆ SCORE

/5☆

WINE Tasting

NAME	
VARIETAL	VINTAGE
PRODUCER	ALCOHOL %
REGION	PRICE
TASTED AT	DATE

👁 APPEARANCE

Color Hue
- ☐ Clear
- ☐ Straw
- ☐ Gold
- ☐ Brown
- ☐ Pink
- ☐ Salmon
- ☐ Orange
- ☐ Brick
- ☐ Ruby
- ☐ Garnet
- ☐ Purple
- ☐

Color Depth
- ☐ Pale
- ☐ Medium
- ☐ Deep

Clarity
- ☐ Clear
- ☐ Hazy
- ☐ Opaque

Viscosity
- ☐ Watery
- ☐ Medium
- ☐ Syrupy

AROMA

☐ Low ☐ Medium ☐ High Intensity

_____
_____
_____
_____
_____
_____
_____

😋 FLAVOR WHEEL

Leather Mushroom
Mineral Woody
Earthy Herbal
Honey Spicy
Dark Fruit Floral
Tropical Fruit Grassy
Smoky Coffee
Nutty Chocolate

TASTE

☐ Sweet	☐ Tart	☐ Light
☐ Medium	☐ Fresh	☐ Medium
☐ Dry	☐ Flabby	☐ Full-Bodied

_____
_____
_____
_____
_____
_____
_____
_____
_____

💬 ADDITIONAL NOTES

_____
_____
_____
_____
_____
_____
_____
_____
_____

FINISH

☐ Short ☐ Medium ☐ Long

_____
_____
_____

🍷 PAIRED WITH

☆ SCORE

/5☆

WINE Tasting

NAME	
VARIETAL	VINTAGE
PRODUCER	ALCOHOL %
REGION	PRICE
TASTED AT	DATE

👁 APPEARANCE

Color Hue
- ☐ Clear
- ☐ Straw
- ☐ Gold
- ☐ Brown
- ☐ Pink
- ☐ Salmon
- ☐ Orange
- ☐ Brick
- ☐ Ruby
- ☐ Garnet
- ☐ Purple
- ☐

Color Depth
- ☐ Pale
- ☐ Medium
- ☐ Deep

Clarity
- ☐ Clear
- ☐ Hazy
- ☐ Opaque

Viscosity
- ☐ Watery
- ☐ Medium
- ☐ Syrupy

AROMA
☐ Low ☐ Medium ☐ High Intensity

_____
_____
_____
_____
_____
_____
_____

TASTE
- ☐ Sweet
- ☐ Medium
- ☐ Dry
- ☐ Tart
- ☐ Fresh
- ☐ Flabby
- ☐ Light
- ☐ Medium
- ☐ Full-Bodied

_____
_____
_____
_____
_____
_____
_____
_____
_____
_____

FINISH
☐ Short ☐ Medium ☐ Long

_____
_____
_____

☺ FLAVOR WHEEL

Leather Mushroom
Mineral Woody
Earthy Herbal
Honey Spicy
Dark Fruit Floral
Tropical Fruit Grassy
Smoky Coffee
Nutty Chocolate

💬 ADDITIONAL NOTES

_____
_____
_____
_____
_____
_____
_____
_____
_____
_____
_____

🍴 PAIRED WITH

☆ SCORE

/5 ☆

22

WINE Tasting

NAME	
VARIETAL	VINTAGE
PRODUCER	ALCOHOL %
REGION	PRICE
TASTED AT	DATE

👁 APPEARANCE

Color Hue
- ☐ Clear
- ☐ Straw
- ☐ Gold
- ☐ Brown
- ☐ Pink
- ☐ Salmon
- ☐ Orange
- ☐ Brick
- ☐ Ruby
- ☐ Garnet
- ☐ Purple
- ☐

Color Depth
- ☐ Pale
- ☐ Medium
- ☐ Deep

Clarity
- ☐ Clear
- ☐ Hazy
- ☐ Opaque

Viscosity
- ☐ Watery
- ☐ Medium
- ☐ Syrupy

AROMA

☐ Low ☐ Medium ☐ High Intensity

_____
_____
_____
_____
_____
_____

😋 FLAVOR WHEEL

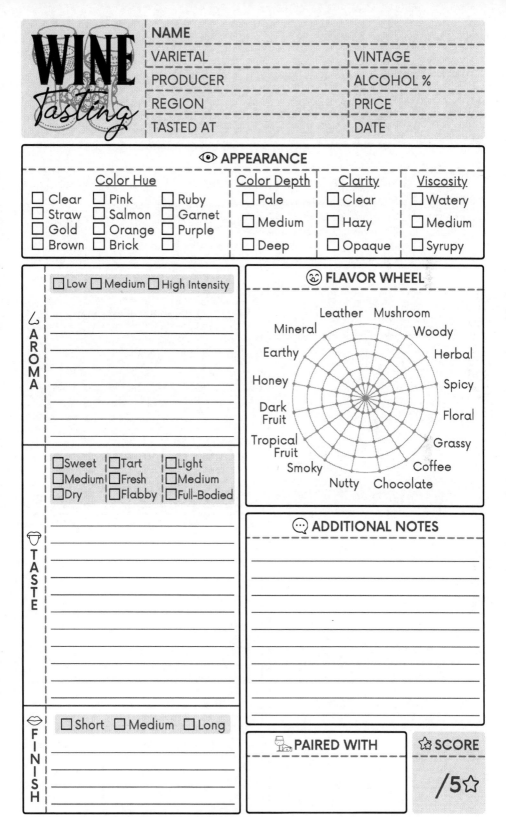

Leather Mushroom
Mineral Woody
Earthy Herbal
Honey Spicy
Dark Fruit Floral
Tropical Fruit Grassy
Smoky Coffee
Nutty Chocolate

TASTE

- ☐ Sweet
- ☐ Medium
- ☐ Dry
- ☐ Tart
- ☐ Fresh
- ☐ Flabby
- ☐ Light
- ☐ Medium
- ☐ Full-Bodied

_____
_____
_____
_____
_____
_____
_____
_____

💬 ADDITIONAL NOTES

_____
_____
_____
_____
_____
_____
_____
_____
_____
_____

FINISH

☐ Short ☐ Medium ☐ Long

_____
_____
_____
_____

🍷 PAIRED WITH

☆ SCORE

/5 ☆

WINE Tasting

NAME	
VARIETAL	VINTAGE
PRODUCER	ALCOHOL %
REGION	PRICE
TASTED AT	DATE

👁 APPEARANCE

Color Hue
- ☐ Clear
- ☐ Straw
- ☐ Gold
- ☐ Brown
- ☐ Pink
- ☐ Salmon
- ☐ Orange
- ☐ Brick
- ☐ Ruby
- ☐ Garnet
- ☐ Purple

Color Depth
- ☐ Pale
- ☐ Medium
- ☐ Deep

Clarity
- ☐ Clear
- ☐ Hazy
- ☐ Opaque

Viscosity
- ☐ Watery
- ☐ Medium
- ☐ Syrupy

AROMA

☐ Low ☐ Medium ☐ High Intensity

_____
_____
_____
_____
_____
_____
_____

😊 FLAVOR WHEEL

Leather   Mushroom
Mineral   Woody
Earthy   Herbal
Honey   Spicy
Dark Fruit   Floral
Tropical Fruit   Grassy
Smoky   Coffee
Nutty   Chocolate

TASTE

- ☐ Sweet
- ☐ Medium
- ☐ Dry
- ☐ Tart
- ☐ Fresh
- ☐ Flabby
- ☐ Light
- ☐ Medium
- ☐ Full-Bodied

_____
_____
_____
_____
_____
_____
_____
_____
_____
_____

💬 ADDITIONAL NOTES

_____
_____
_____
_____
_____
_____
_____
_____
_____
_____

FINISH

☐ Short ☐ Medium ☐ Long

_____
_____
_____

🍷 PAIRED WITH

☆ SCORE

/5☆

WINE Tasting

NAME	
VARIETAL	VINTAGE
PRODUCER	ALCOHOL %
REGION	PRICE
TASTED AT	DATE

👁 APPEARANCE

Color Hue
- ☐ Clear
- ☐ Straw
- ☐ Gold
- ☐ Brown
- ☐ Pink
- ☐ Salmon
- ☐ Orange
- ☐ Brick
- ☐ Ruby
- ☐ Garnet
- ☐ Purple
- ☐

Color Depth
- ☐ Pale
- ☐ Medium
- ☐ Deep

Clarity
- ☐ Clear
- ☐ Hazy
- ☐ Opaque

Viscosity
- ☐ Watery
- ☐ Medium
- ☐ Syrupy

AROMA

☐ Low ☐ Medium ☐ High Intensity

TASTE

- ☐ Sweet
- ☐ Medium
- ☐ Dry
- ☐ Tart
- ☐ Fresh
- ☐ Flabby
- ☐ Light
- ☐ Medium
- ☐ Full-Bodied

FINISH

☐ Short ☐ Medium ☐ Long

😋 FLAVOR WHEEL

Leather Mushroom
Mineral Woody
Earthy Herbal
Honey Spicy
Dark Fruit Floral
Tropical Fruit Grassy
Smoky Coffee
Nutty Chocolate

💬 ADDITIONAL NOTES

🍷 PAIRED WITH

☆ SCORE

/5 ☆

25

WINE Tasting

NAME	
VARIETAL	VINTAGE
PRODUCER	ALCOHOL %
REGION	PRICE
TASTED AT	DATE

👁 APPEARANCE

Color Hue
- ☐ Clear
- ☐ Straw
- ☐ Gold
- ☐ Brown
- ☐ Pink
- ☐ Salmon
- ☐ Orange
- ☐ Brick
- ☐ Ruby
- ☐ Garnet
- ☐ Purple
- ☐

Color Depth
- ☐ Pale
- ☐ Medium
- ☐ Deep

Clarity
- ☐ Clear
- ☐ Hazy
- ☐ Opaque

Viscosity
- ☐ Watery
- ☐ Medium
- ☐ Syrupy

AROMA

☐ Low ☐ Medium ☐ High Intensity

_____
_____
_____
_____
_____
_____
_____
_____

TASTE

☐ Sweet ☐ Tart ☐ Light
☐ Medium ☐ Fresh ☐ Medium
☐ Dry ☐ Flabby ☐ Full-Bodied

_____
_____
_____
_____
_____
_____
_____
_____
_____
_____

FINISH

☐ Short ☐ Medium ☐ Long

_____
_____
_____

😋 FLAVOR WHEEL

Leather Mushroom
Mineral Woody
Earthy Herbal
Honey Spicy
Dark Fruit Floral
Tropical Fruit Grassy
Smoky Coffee
Nutty Chocolate

💬 ADDITIONAL NOTES

_____
_____
_____
_____
_____
_____
_____
_____
_____
_____
_____
_____

🍽 PAIRED WITH

☆ SCORE

/5☆

WINE Tasting

NAME	
VARIETAL	VINTAGE
PRODUCER	ALCOHOL %
REGION	PRICE
TASTED AT	DATE

👁 APPEARANCE

Color Hue
- ☐ Clear
- ☐ Straw
- ☐ Gold
- ☐ Brown
- ☐ Pink
- ☐ Salmon
- ☐ Orange
- ☐ Brick
- ☐ Ruby
- ☐ Garnet
- ☐ Purple
- ☐

Color Depth
- ☐ Pale
- ☐ Medium
- ☐ Deep

Clarity
- ☐ Clear
- ☐ Hazy
- ☐ Opaque

Viscosity
- ☐ Watery
- ☐ Medium
- ☐ Syrupy

AROMA

☐ Low ☐ Medium ☐ High Intensity

_____
_____
_____
_____
_____
_____

TASTE

- ☐ Sweet
- ☐ Medium
- ☐ Dry
- ☐ Tart
- ☐ Fresh
- ☐ Flabby
- ☐ Light
- ☐ Medium
- ☐ Full-Bodied

_____
_____
_____
_____
_____
_____
_____
_____

FINISH

☐ Short ☐ Medium ☐ Long

_____
_____
_____
_____

😋 FLAVOR WHEEL

Leather Mushroom
Mineral Woody
Earthy Herbal
Honey Spicy
Dark Fruit Floral
Tropical Fruit Grassy
Smoky Coffee
Nutty Chocolate

💬 ADDITIONAL NOTES

_____
_____
_____
_____
_____
_____
_____
_____
_____
_____
_____

🍷 PAIRED WITH

☆ SCORE

/5 ☆

WINE Tasting

NAME	
VARIETAL	VINTAGE
PRODUCER	ALCOHOL %
REGION	PRICE
TASTED AT	DATE

👁 APPEARANCE

Color Hue
- ☐ Clear
- ☐ Straw
- ☐ Gold
- ☐ Brown
- ☐ Pink
- ☐ Salmon
- ☐ Orange
- ☐ Brick
- ☐ Ruby
- ☐ Garnet
- ☐ Purple
- ☐

Color Depth
- ☐ Pale
- ☐ Medium
- ☐ Deep

Clarity
- ☐ Clear
- ☐ Hazy
- ☐ Opaque

Viscosity
- ☐ Watery
- ☐ Medium
- ☐ Syrupy

AROMA

☐ Low ☐ Medium ☐ High Intensity

_____
_____
_____
_____
_____
_____
_____

TASTE

- ☐ Sweet
- ☐ Medium
- ☐ Dry
- ☐ Tart
- ☐ Fresh
- ☐ Flabby
- ☐ Light
- ☐ Medium
- ☐ Full-Bodied

_____
_____
_____
_____
_____
_____
_____
_____
_____
_____
_____

FINISH

☐ Short ☐ Medium ☐ Long

_____
_____
_____

😋 FLAVOR WHEEL

Leather Mushroom
Mineral Woody
Earthy Herbal
Honey Spicy
Dark Fruit Floral
Tropical Fruit Grassy
Smoky Coffee
Nutty Chocolate

💬 ADDITIONAL NOTES

_____
_____
_____
_____
_____
_____
_____
_____
_____
_____

🍷 PAIRED WITH

☆ SCORE

/5 ☆

WINE Tasting

NAME	
VARIETAL	VINTAGE
PRODUCER	ALCOHOL %
REGION	PRICE
TASTED AT	DATE

👁 APPEARANCE

Color Hue
- ☐ Clear
- ☐ Straw
- ☐ Gold
- ☐ Brown
- ☐ Pink
- ☐ Salmon
- ☐ Orange
- ☐ Brick
- ☐ Ruby
- ☐ Garnet
- ☐ Purple

Color Depth
- ☐ Pale
- ☐ Medium
- ☐ Deep

Clarity
- ☐ Clear
- ☐ Hazy
- ☐ Opaque

Viscosity
- ☐ Watery
- ☐ Medium
- ☐ Syrupy

AROMA
☐ Low ☐ Medium ☐ High Intensity

_____
_____
_____
_____
_____
_____

TASTE
- ☐ Sweet
- ☐ Medium
- ☐ Dry
- ☐ Tart
- ☐ Fresh
- ☐ Flabby
- ☐ Light
- ☐ Medium
- ☐ Full-Bodied

_____
_____
_____
_____
_____
_____
_____
_____
_____

FINISH
☐ Short ☐ Medium ☐ Long

_____
_____
_____

😊 FLAVOR WHEEL

Leather Mushroom
Mineral Woody
Earthy Herbal
Honey Spicy
Dark Fruit Floral
Tropical Fruit Grassy
Smoky Coffee
Nutty Chocolate

💬 ADDITIONAL NOTES

_____
_____
_____
_____
_____
_____
_____
_____
_____
_____
_____

🍷 PAIRED WITH

☆ SCORE

/5 ☆

WINE Tasting

NAME	
VARIETAL	VINTAGE
PRODUCER	ALCOHOL %
REGION	PRICE
TASTED AT	DATE

👁 APPEARANCE

Color Hue
☐ Clear ☐ Pink ☐ Ruby
☐ Straw ☐ Salmon ☐ Garnet
☐ Gold ☐ Orange ☐ Purple
☐ Brown ☐ Brick ☐

Color Depth
☐ Pale
☐ Medium
☐ Deep

Clarity
☐ Clear
☐ Hazy
☐ Opaque

Viscosity
☐ Watery
☐ Medium
☐ Syrupy

AROMA
☐ Low ☐ Medium ☐ High Intensity

_____
_____
_____
_____
_____
_____

TASTE
☐ Sweet ☐ Tart ☐ Light
☐ Medium ☐ Fresh ☐ Medium
☐ Dry ☐ Flabby ☐ Full-Bodied

_____
_____
_____
_____
_____
_____
_____
_____

FINISH
☐ Short ☐ Medium ☐ Long

_____
_____
_____

😊 FLAVOR WHEEL

Leather Mushroom
Mineral Woody
Earthy Herbal
Honey Spicy
Dark Fruit Floral
Tropical Fruit Grassy
Smoky Coffee
Nutty Chocolate

💬 ADDITIONAL NOTES

_____
_____
_____
_____
_____
_____
_____
_____
_____
_____
_____

🍷 PAIRED WITH

☆ SCORE

/5 ☆

WINE Tasting

NAME	
VARIETAL	VINTAGE
PRODUCER	ALCOHOL %
REGION	PRICE
TASTED AT	DATE

👁 APPEARANCE

Color Hue
☐ Clear ☐ Pink ☐ Ruby
☐ Straw ☐ Salmon ☐ Garnet
☐ Gold ☐ Orange ☐ Purple
☐ Brown ☐ Brick ☐

Color Depth
☐ Pale
☐ Medium
☐ Deep

Clarity
☐ Clear
☐ Hazy
☐ Opaque

Viscosity
☐ Watery
☐ Medium
☐ Syrupy

AROMA

☐ Low ☐ Medium ☐ High Intensity

_____
_____
_____
_____
_____
_____

TASTE

☐ Sweet ☐ Tart ☐ Light
☐ Medium ☐ Fresh ☐ Medium
☐ Dry ☐ Flabby ☐ Full-Bodied

_____
_____
_____
_____
_____
_____
_____
_____

FINISH

☐ Short ☐ Medium ☐ Long

_____
_____
_____

😋 FLAVOR WHEEL

Leather Mushroom
Mineral Woody
Earthy Herbal
Honey Spicy
Dark Fruit Floral
Tropical Fruit Grassy
Smoky Coffee
Nutty Chocolate

💬 ADDITIONAL NOTES

_____
_____
_____
_____
_____
_____
_____
_____
_____

🍷 PAIRED WITH

☆ SCORE

/5☆

WINE Tasting

NAME	
VARIETAL	VINTAGE
PRODUCER	ALCOHOL %
REGION	PRICE
TASTED AT	DATE

👁 APPEARANCE

Color Hue
- ☐ Clear
- ☐ Straw
- ☐ Gold
- ☐ Brown
- ☐ Pink
- ☐ Salmon
- ☐ Orange
- ☐ Brick
- ☐ Ruby
- ☐ Garnet
- ☐ Purple

Color Depth
- ☐ Pale
- ☐ Medium
- ☐ Deep

Clarity
- ☐ Clear
- ☐ Hazy
- ☐ Opaque

Viscosity
- ☐ Watery
- ☐ Medium
- ☐ Syrupy

AROMA
☐ Low ☐ Medium ☐ High Intensity

_____
_____
_____
_____
_____

TASTE
- ☐ Sweet
- ☐ Medium
- ☐ Dry
- ☐ Tart
- ☐ Fresh
- ☐ Flabby
- ☐ Light
- ☐ Medium
- ☐ Full-Bodied

_____
_____
_____
_____
_____
_____
_____
_____

FINISH
☐ Short ☐ Medium ☐ Long

_____
_____
_____

😋 FLAVOR WHEEL

Leather Mushroom
Mineral Woody
Earthy Herbal
Honey Spicy
Dark Fruit Floral
Tropical Fruit Grassy
Smoky Coffee
Nutty Chocolate

💬 ADDITIONAL NOTES

_____
_____
_____
_____
_____
_____
_____
_____
_____
_____
_____

🍷 PAIRED WITH

⭐ SCORE

/5 ☆

WINE Tasting

NAME	
VARIETAL	VINTAGE
PRODUCER	ALCOHOL %
REGION	PRICE
TASTED AT	DATE

👁 APPEARANCE

Color Hue
- ☐ Clear
- ☐ Straw
- ☐ Gold
- ☐ Brown
- ☐ Pink
- ☐ Salmon
- ☐ Orange
- ☐ Brick
- ☐ Ruby
- ☐ Garnet
- ☐ Purple
- ☐

Color Depth
- ☐ Pale
- ☐ Medium
- ☐ Deep

Clarity
- ☐ Clear
- ☐ Hazy
- ☐ Opaque

Viscosity
- ☐ Watery
- ☐ Medium
- ☐ Syrupy

AROMA

☐ Low ☐ Medium ☐ High Intensity

_____
_____
_____
_____
_____
_____

☺ FLAVOR WHEEL

Leather   Mushroom
Mineral   Woody
Earthy   Herbal
Honey   Spicy
Dark Fruit   Floral
Tropical Fruit   Grassy
Smoky   Coffee
Nutty   Chocolate

TASTE

- ☐ Sweet
- ☐ Medium
- ☐ Dry
- ☐ Tart
- ☐ Fresh
- ☐ Flabby
- ☐ Light
- ☐ Medium
- ☐ Full-Bodied

_____
_____
_____
_____
_____
_____
_____
_____
_____

💬 ADDITIONAL NOTES

_____
_____
_____
_____
_____
_____
_____
_____
_____
_____
_____

FINISH

☐ Short ☐ Medium ☐ Long

_____
_____
_____
_____

🍷 PAIRED WITH

☆ SCORE

/5 ☆

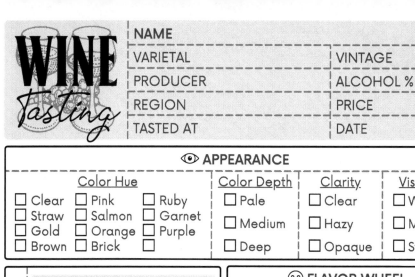

WINE Tasting

NAME	
VARIETAL	VINTAGE
PRODUCER	ALCOHOL %
REGION	PRICE
TASTED AT	DATE

👁 APPEARANCE

Color Hue			Color Depth	Clarity	Viscosity
☐ Clear	☐ Pink	☐ Ruby	☐ Pale	☐ Clear	☐ Watery
☐ Straw	☐ Salmon	☐ Garnet	☐ Medium	☐ Hazy	☐ Medium
☐ Gold	☐ Orange	☐ Purple	☐ Deep	☐ Opaque	☐ Syrupy
☐ Brown	☐ Brick	☐			

AROMA

☐ Low ☐ Medium ☐ High Intensity

_____
_____
_____
_____
_____
_____
_____

😋 FLAVOR WHEEL

Leather   Mushroom
Mineral   Woody
Earthy   Herbal
Honey   Spicy
Dark Fruit   Floral
Tropical Fruit   Grassy
Smoky   Coffee
Nutty   Chocolate

TASTE

☐ Sweet ☐ Tart ☐ Light
☐ Medium ☐ Fresh ☐ Medium
☐ Dry ☐ Flabby ☐ Full-Bodied

_____
_____
_____
_____
_____
_____
_____
_____
_____

💬 ADDITIONAL NOTES

_____
_____
_____
_____
_____
_____
_____
_____
_____
_____

FINISH

☐ Short ☐ Medium ☐ Long

_____
_____
_____

🍷 PAIRED WITH

☆ SCORE

/5 ☆

WINE Tasting

NAME	
VARIETAL	VINTAGE
PRODUCER	ALCOHOL %
REGION	PRICE
TASTED AT	DATE

👁 APPEARANCE

Color Hue
- ☐ Clear
- ☐ Straw
- ☐ Gold
- ☐ Brown
- ☐ Pink
- ☐ Salmon
- ☐ Orange
- ☐ Brick
- ☐ Ruby
- ☐ Garnet
- ☐ Purple
- ☐

Color Depth
- ☐ Pale
- ☐ Medium
- ☐ Deep

Clarity
- ☐ Clear
- ☐ Hazy
- ☐ Opaque

Viscosity
- ☐ Watery
- ☐ Medium
- ☐ Syrupy

AROMA

☐ Low ☐ Medium ☐ High Intensity

_____
_____
_____
_____
_____
_____
_____
_____

😋 FLAVOR WHEEL

Leather Mushroom
Mineral Woody
Earthy Herbal
Honey Spicy
Dark Fruit Floral
Tropical Fruit Grassy
Smoky Coffee
Nutty Chocolate

TASTE

- ☐ Sweet
- ☐ Medium
- ☐ Dry
- ☐ Tart
- ☐ Fresh
- ☐ Flabby
- ☐ Light
- ☐ Medium
- ☐ Full-Bodied

_____
_____
_____
_____
_____
_____
_____
_____
_____

💬 ADDITIONAL NOTES

_____
_____
_____
_____
_____
_____
_____
_____
_____
_____
_____
_____

FINISH

☐ Short ☐ Medium ☐ Long

_____
_____
_____

🍷 PAIRED WITH

☆ SCORE

/5 ☆

WINE Tasting

NAME	
VARIETAL	VINTAGE
PRODUCER	ALCOHOL %
REGION	PRICE
TASTED AT	DATE

👁 APPEARANCE

Color Hue
☐ Clear ☐ Pink ☐ Ruby
☐ Straw ☐ Salmon ☐ Garnet
☐ Gold ☐ Orange ☐ Purple
☐ Brown ☐ Brick ☐

Color Depth
☐ Pale
☐ Medium
☐ Deep

Clarity
☐ Clear
☐ Hazy
☐ Opaque

Viscosity
☐ Watery
☐ Medium
☐ Syrupy

AROMA

☐ Low ☐ Medium ☐ High Intensity

_____
_____
_____
_____
_____
_____
_____

😋 FLAVOR WHEEL

Leather Mushroom
Mineral Woody
Earthy Herbal
Honey Spicy
Dark Fruit Floral
Tropical Fruit Grassy
Smoky Coffee
Nutty Chocolate

TASTE

☐ Sweet ☐ Tart ☐ Light
☐ Medium ☐ Fresh ☐ Medium
☐ Dry ☐ Flabby ☐ Full-Bodied

_____
_____
_____
_____
_____
_____
_____
_____
_____

💬 ADDITIONAL NOTES

_____
_____
_____
_____
_____
_____
_____
_____
_____
_____
_____

FINISH

☐ Short ☐ Medium ☐ Long

_____
_____
_____

🍷 PAIRED WITH

☆ SCORE

/5 ☆

WINE Tasting

NAME	
VARIETAL	**VINTAGE**
PRODUCER	**ALCOHOL %**
REGION	**PRICE**
TASTED AT	**DATE**

👁 APPEARANCE

Color Hue
- ☐ Clear
- ☐ Straw
- ☐ Gold
- ☐ Brown
- ☐ Pink
- ☐ Salmon
- ☐ Orange
- ☐ Brick
- ☐ Ruby
- ☐ Garnet
- ☐ Purple
- ☐

Color Depth
- ☐ Pale
- ☐ Medium
- ☐ Deep

Clarity
- ☐ Clear
- ☐ Hazy
- ☐ Opaque

Viscosity
- ☐ Watery
- ☐ Medium
- ☐ Syrupy

AROMA

☐ Low ☐ Medium ☐ High Intensity

_____
_____
_____
_____
_____

TASTE

- ☐ Sweet
- ☐ Medium
- ☐ Dry
- ☐ Tart
- ☐ Fresh
- ☐ Flabby
- ☐ Light
- ☐ Medium
- ☐ Full-Bodied

_____
_____
_____
_____
_____
_____
_____

FINISH

☐ Short ☐ Medium ☐ Long

_____
_____
_____

😋 FLAVOR WHEEL

Leather Mushroom
Mineral Woody
Earthy Herbal
Honey Spicy
Dark Fruit Floral
Tropical Fruit Grassy
Smoky Coffee
Nutty Chocolate

💬 ADDITIONAL NOTES

_____
_____
_____
_____
_____
_____
_____
_____
_____
_____

🍷 PAIRED WITH

☆ SCORE

/5☆

WINE Tasting

NAME	
VARIETAL	VINTAGE
PRODUCER	ALCOHOL %
REGION	PRICE
TASTED AT	DATE

👁 APPEARANCE

Color Hue
- ☐ Clear
- ☐ Straw
- ☐ Gold
- ☐ Brown
- ☐ Pink
- ☐ Salmon
- ☐ Orange
- ☐ Brick
- ☐ Ruby
- ☐ Garnet
- ☐ Purple
- ☐

Color Depth
- ☐ Pale
- ☐ Medium
- ☐ Deep

Clarity
- ☐ Clear
- ☐ Hazy
- ☐ Opaque

Viscosity
- ☐ Watery
- ☐ Medium
- ☐ Syrupy

AROMA

☐ Low ☐ Medium ☐ High Intensity

_____
_____
_____
_____
_____
_____
_____

😋 FLAVOR WHEEL

Leather Mushroom
Mineral Woody
Earthy Herbal
Honey Spicy
Dark Fruit Floral
Tropical Fruit Grassy
Smoky Coffee
Nutty Chocolate

TASTE

- ☐ Sweet
- ☐ Medium
- ☐ Dry
- ☐ Tart
- ☐ Fresh
- ☐ Flabby
- ☐ Light
- ☐ Medium
- ☐ Full-Bodied

_____
_____
_____
_____
_____
_____
_____
_____
_____

💬 ADDITIONAL NOTES

_____
_____
_____
_____
_____
_____
_____
_____
_____
_____

FINISH

☐ Short ☐ Medium ☐ Long

_____
_____
_____

🍷 PAIRED WITH

☆ SCORE

/5 ☆

WINE Tasting

NAME	
VARIETAL	VINTAGE
PRODUCER	ALCOHOL %
REGION	PRICE
TASTED AT	DATE

👁 APPEARANCE

Color Hue
- ☐ Clear
- ☐ Straw
- ☐ Gold
- ☐ Brown
- ☐ Pink
- ☐ Salmon
- ☐ Orange
- ☐ Brick
- ☐ Ruby
- ☐ Garnet
- ☐ Purple
- ☐

Color Depth
- ☐ Pale
- ☐ Medium
- ☐ Deep

Clarity
- ☐ Clear
- ☐ Hazy
- ☐ Opaque

Viscosity
- ☐ Watery
- ☐ Medium
- ☐ Syrupy

AROMA
☐ Low ☐ Medium ☐ High Intensity
_____
_____
_____
_____
_____
_____
_____

TASTE
- ☐ Sweet
- ☐ Medium
- ☐ Dry
- ☐ Tart
- ☐ Fresh
- ☐ Flabby
- ☐ Light
- ☐ Medium
- ☐ Full-Bodied

_____
_____
_____
_____
_____
_____
_____
_____
_____
_____

FINISH
☐ Short ☐ Medium ☐ Long
_____
_____
_____

😋 FLAVOR WHEEL

Leather Mushroom
Mineral   Woody
Earthy   Herbal
Honey   Spicy
Dark Fruit   Floral
Tropical Fruit   Grassy
Smoky   Coffee
Nutty   Chocolate

💬 ADDITIONAL NOTES
_____
_____
_____
_____
_____
_____
_____
_____
_____
_____
_____
_____
_____

🍷 PAIRED WITH

☆ SCORE
/5 ☆

NAME

VARIETAL	VINTAGE
PRODUCER	ALCOHOL %
REGION	PRICE
TASTED AT	DATE

👁 APPEARANCE

Color Hue			Color Depth	Clarity	Viscosity
☐ Clear	☐ Pink	☐ Ruby	☐ Pale	☐ Clear	☐ Watery
☐ Straw	☐ Salmon	☐ Garnet	☐ Medium	☐ Hazy	☐ Medium
☐ Gold	☐ Orange	☐ Purple			
☐ Brown	☐ Brick	☐	☐ Deep	☐ Opaque	☐ Syrupy

AROMA

☐ Low ☐ Medium ☐ High Intensity

_____
_____
_____
_____
_____
_____
_____
_____

TASTE

☐ Sweet ☐ Tart ☐ Light
☐ Medium ☐ Fresh ☐ Medium
☐ Dry ☐ Flabby ☐ Full-Bodied

_____
_____
_____
_____
_____
_____
_____
_____
_____
_____
_____

FINISH

☐ Short ☐ Medium ☐ Long

_____
_____
_____

😋 FLAVOR WHEEL

Leather Mushroom
Mineral Woody
Earthy Herbal
Honey Spicy
Dark Fruit Floral
Tropical Fruit Grassy
Smoky Coffee
Nutty Chocolate

💬 ADDITIONAL NOTES

_____
_____
_____
_____
_____
_____
_____
_____
_____
_____

🍷 PAIRED WITH

⭐ SCORE

/5 ☆

WINE Tasting

NAME	
VARIETAL	VINTAGE
PRODUCER	ALCOHOL %
REGION	PRICE
TASTED AT	DATE

👁 APPEARANCE

Color Hue			Color Depth	Clarity	Viscosity
☐ Clear	☐ Pink	☐ Ruby	☐ Pale	☐ Clear	☐ Watery
☐ Straw	☐ Salmon	☐ Garnet	☐ Medium	☐ Hazy	☐ Medium
☐ Gold	☐ Orange	☐ Purple	☐ Deep	☐ Opaque	☐ Syrupy
☐ Brown	☐ Brick	☐			

AROMA

☐ Low ☐ Medium ☐ High Intensity

_____
_____
_____
_____
_____
_____

😋 FLAVOR WHEEL

Leather Mushroom
Mineral Woody
Earthy Herbal
Honey Spicy
Dark Fruit Floral
Tropical Fruit Grassy
Smoky Coffee
Nutty Chocolate

TASTE

☐ Sweet ☐ Tart ☐ Light
☐ Medium ☐ Fresh ☐ Medium
☐ Dry ☐ Flabby ☐ Full-Bodied

_____
_____
_____
_____
_____
_____
_____
_____
_____
_____

💬 ADDITIONAL NOTES

_____
_____
_____
_____
_____
_____
_____
_____
_____
_____
_____

FINISH

☐ Short ☐ Medium ☐ Long

_____
_____
_____

🍷 PAIRED WITH

⭐ SCORE

/5☆

WINE Tasting

NAME	
VARIETAL	VINTAGE
PRODUCER	ALCOHOL %
REGION	PRICE
TASTED AT	DATE

👁 APPEARANCE

Color Hue
- ☐ Clear
- ☐ Straw
- ☐ Gold
- ☐ Brown
- ☐ Pink
- ☐ Salmon
- ☐ Orange
- ☐ Brick
- ☐ Ruby
- ☐ Garnet
- ☐ Purple
- ☐

Color Depth
- ☐ Pale
- ☐ Medium
- ☐ Deep

Clarity
- ☐ Clear
- ☐ Hazy
- ☐ Opaque

Viscosity
- ☐ Watery
- ☐ Medium
- ☐ Syrupy

AROMA
☐ Low ☐ Medium ☐ High Intensity

_____
_____
_____
_____
_____
_____
_____

TASTE
- ☐ Sweet
- ☐ Medium
- ☐ Dry
- ☐ Tart
- ☐ Fresh
- ☐ Flabby
- ☐ Light
- ☐ Medium
- ☐ Full-Bodied

_____
_____
_____
_____
_____
_____
_____
_____
_____

FINISH
☐ Short ☐ Medium ☐ Long

_____
_____
_____

😋 FLAVOR WHEEL

Leather   Mushroom
Mineral   Woody
Earthy   Herbal
Honey   Spicy
Dark Fruit   Floral
Tropical Fruit   Grassy
Smoky   Coffee
Nutty   Chocolate

💬 ADDITIONAL NOTES

_____
_____
_____
_____
_____
_____
_____
_____
_____
_____
_____
_____

🍽 PAIRED WITH

☆ SCORE

/5 ☆

42

WINE Tasting

NAME	
VARIETAL	VINTAGE
PRODUCER	ALCOHOL %
REGION	PRICE
TASTED AT	DATE

👁 APPEARANCE

Color Hue
- ☐ Clear
- ☐ Straw
- ☐ Gold
- ☐ Brown
- ☐ Pink
- ☐ Salmon
- ☐ Orange
- ☐ Brick
- ☐ Ruby
- ☐ Garnet
- ☐ Purple
- ☐

Color Depth
- ☐ Pale
- ☐ Medium
- ☐ Deep

Clarity
- ☐ Clear
- ☐ Hazy
- ☐ Opaque

Viscosity
- ☐ Watery
- ☐ Medium
- ☐ Syrupy

AROMA

☐ Low ☐ Medium ☐ High Intensity

_____
_____
_____
_____
_____
_____

TASTE

- ☐ Sweet
- ☐ Medium
- ☐ Dry
- ☐ Tart
- ☐ Fresh
- ☐ Flabby
- ☐ Light
- ☐ Medium
- ☐ Full-Bodied

_____
_____
_____
_____
_____
_____
_____
_____

FINISH

☐ Short ☐ Medium ☐ Long

_____
_____
_____

😋 FLAVOR WHEEL

Leather Mushroom
Mineral Woody
Earthy Herbal
Honey Spicy
Dark Fruit Floral
Tropical Fruit Grassy
Smoky Coffee
Nutty Chocolate

💬 ADDITIONAL NOTES

_____
_____
_____
_____
_____
_____
_____
_____
_____
_____
_____

🍷 PAIRED WITH

☆ SCORE

/5 ☆

WINE Tasting

NAME	
VARIETAL	VINTAGE
PRODUCER	ALCOHOL %
REGION	PRICE
TASTED AT	DATE

👁 APPEARANCE

Color Hue
- ☐ Clear
- ☐ Straw
- ☐ Gold
- ☐ Brown
- ☐ Pink
- ☐ Salmon
- ☐ Orange
- ☐ Brick
- ☐ Ruby
- ☐ Garnet
- ☐ Purple
- ☐

Color Depth
- ☐ Pale
- ☐ Medium
- ☐ Deep

Clarity
- ☐ Clear
- ☐ Hazy
- ☐ Opaque

Viscosity
- ☐ Watery
- ☐ Medium
- ☐ Syrupy

AROMA

☐ Low ☐ Medium ☐ High Intensity

_____
_____
_____
_____
_____
_____
_____

😊 FLAVOR WHEEL

Leather Mushroom
Mineral   Woody
Earthy   Herbal
Honey   Spicy
Dark Fruit   Floral
Tropical Fruit   Grassy
Smoky   Coffee
Nutty Chocolate

TASTE

- ☐ Sweet
- ☐ Medium
- ☐ Dry
- ☐ Tart
- ☐ Fresh
- ☐ Flabby
- ☐ Light
- ☐ Medium
- ☐ Full-Bodied

_____
_____
_____
_____
_____
_____
_____
_____
_____

💬 ADDITIONAL NOTES

_____
_____
_____
_____
_____
_____
_____
_____
_____
_____
_____

FINISH

☐ Short ☐ Medium ☐ Long

_____
_____
_____

🍷 PAIRED WITH

☆ SCORE

/5 ☆

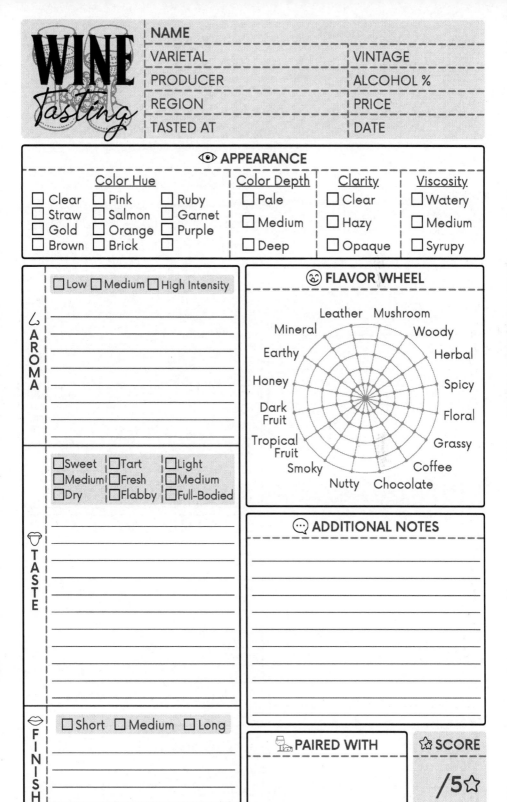

WINE Tasting

NAME	
VARIETAL	VINTAGE
PRODUCER	ALCOHOL %
REGION	PRICE
TASTED AT	DATE

👁 APPEARANCE

Color Hue
- ☐ Clear
- ☐ Straw
- ☐ Gold
- ☐ Brown
- ☐ Pink
- ☐ Salmon
- ☐ Orange
- ☐ Brick
- ☐ Ruby
- ☐ Garnet
- ☐ Purple
- ☐

Color Depth
- ☐ Pale
- ☐ Medium
- ☐ Deep

Clarity
- ☐ Clear
- ☐ Hazy
- ☐ Opaque

Viscosity
- ☐ Watery
- ☐ Medium
- ☐ Syrupy

AROMA

☐ Low ☐ Medium ☐ High Intensity

_____
_____
_____
_____
_____
_____
_____

TASTE

- ☐ Sweet
- ☐ Medium
- ☐ Dry
- ☐ Tart
- ☐ Fresh
- ☐ Flabby
- ☐ Light
- ☐ Medium
- ☐ Full-Bodied

_____
_____
_____
_____
_____
_____
_____
_____
_____

FINISH

☐ Short ☐ Medium ☐ Long

_____
_____
_____

😋 FLAVOR WHEEL

Leather Mushroom
Mineral Woody
Earthy Herbal
Honey Spicy
Dark Fruit Floral
Tropical Fruit Grassy
Smoky Coffee
Nutty Chocolate

💬 ADDITIONAL NOTES

_____
_____
_____
_____
_____
_____
_____
_____
_____
_____

🍷 PAIRED WITH

☆ SCORE

/5 ☆

45

WINE Tasting

NAME	
VARIETAL	VINTAGE
PRODUCER	ALCOHOL %
REGION	PRICE
TASTED AT	DATE

👁 APPEARANCE

Color Hue
- ☐ Clear
- ☐ Straw
- ☐ Gold
- ☐ Brown
- ☐ Pink
- ☐ Salmon
- ☐ Orange
- ☐ Brick
- ☐ Ruby
- ☐ Garnet
- ☐ Purple
- ☐

Color Depth
- ☐ Pale
- ☐ Medium
- ☐ Deep

Clarity
- ☐ Clear
- ☐ Hazy
- ☐ Opaque

Viscosity
- ☐ Watery
- ☐ Medium
- ☐ Syrupy

AROMA

☐ Low ☐ Medium ☐ High Intensity

_____
_____
_____
_____
_____
_____
_____

TASTE

☐ Sweet ☐ Tart ☐ Light
☐ Medium ☐ Fresh ☐ Medium
☐ Dry ☐ Flabby ☐ Full-Bodied

_____
_____
_____
_____
_____
_____
_____
_____
_____
_____

FINISH

☐ Short ☐ Medium ☐ Long

_____
_____
_____

😋 FLAVOR WHEEL

Leather Mushroom
Mineral Woody
Earthy Herbal
Honey Spicy
Dark Fruit Floral
Tropical Fruit Grassy
Smoky Coffee
Nutty Chocolate

💬 ADDITIONAL NOTES

_____
_____
_____
_____
_____
_____
_____
_____
_____
_____
_____

🍷 PAIRED WITH

⭐ SCORE

/5 ☆

WINE Tasting

NAME	
VARIETAL	VINTAGE
PRODUCER	ALCOHOL %
REGION	PRICE
TASTED AT	DATE

👁 APPEARANCE

Color Hue
- ☐ Clear
- ☐ Straw
- ☐ Gold
- ☐ Brown
- ☐ Pink
- ☐ Salmon
- ☐ Orange
- ☐ Brick
- ☐ Ruby
- ☐ Garnet
- ☐ Purple

Color Depth
- ☐ Pale
- ☐ Medium
- ☐ Deep

Clarity
- ☐ Clear
- ☐ Hazy
- ☐ Opaque

Viscosity
- ☐ Watery
- ☐ Medium
- ☐ Syrupy

AROMA

☐ Low ☐ Medium ☐ High Intensity

_____
_____
_____
_____
_____
_____
_____

TASTE

- ☐ Sweet
- ☐ Medium
- ☐ Dry
- ☐ Tart
- ☐ Fresh
- ☐ Flabby
- ☐ Light
- ☐ Medium
- ☐ Full-Bodied

_____
_____
_____
_____
_____
_____
_____
_____
_____

FINISH

☐ Short ☐ Medium ☐ Long

_____
_____
_____

😋 FLAVOR WHEEL

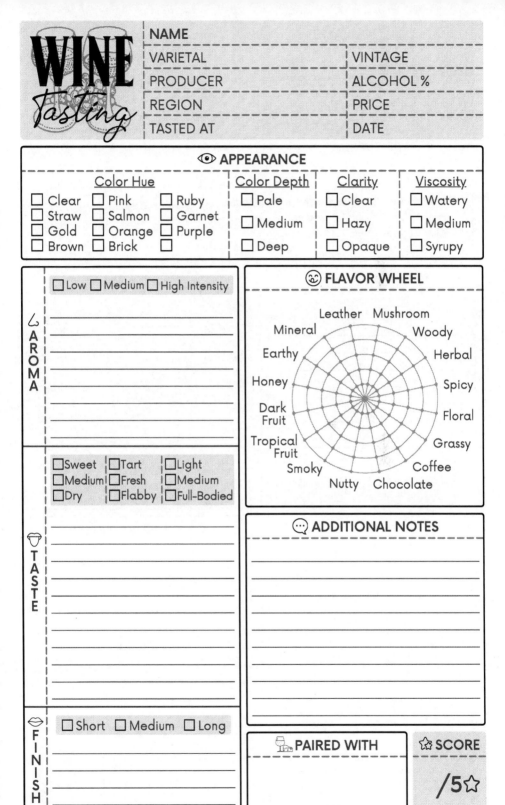

Leather Mushroom
Mineral Woody
Earthy Herbal
Honey Spicy
Dark Fruit Floral
Tropical Fruit Grassy
Smoky Coffee
Nutty Chocolate

💬 ADDITIONAL NOTES

_____
_____
_____
_____
_____
_____
_____
_____
_____
_____
_____

🍷 PAIRED WITH

☆ SCORE

/5☆

47

WINE Tasting

NAME	
VARIETAL	VINTAGE
PRODUCER	ALCOHOL %
REGION	PRICE
TASTED AT	DATE

👁 APPEARANCE

Color Hue
- ☐ Clear
- ☐ Straw
- ☐ Gold
- ☐ Brown
- ☐ Pink
- ☐ Salmon
- ☐ Orange
- ☐ Brick
- ☐ Ruby
- ☐ Garnet
- ☐ Purple

Color Depth
- ☐ Pale
- ☐ Medium
- ☐ Deep

Clarity
- ☐ Clear
- ☐ Hazy
- ☐ Opaque

Viscosity
- ☐ Watery
- ☐ Medium
- ☐ Syrupy

AROMA

☐ Low ☐ Medium ☐ High Intensity

_____
_____
_____
_____
_____
_____
_____
_____

TASTE

- ☐ Sweet
- ☐ Medium
- ☐ Dry
- ☐ Tart
- ☐ Fresh
- ☐ Flabby
- ☐ Light
- ☐ Medium
- ☐ Full-Bodied

_____
_____
_____
_____
_____
_____
_____
_____
_____

FINISH

☐ Short ☐ Medium ☐ Long

_____
_____
_____

😊 FLAVOR WHEEL

Leather Mushroom
Mineral Woody
Earthy Herbal
Honey Spicy
Dark Fruit Floral
Tropical Fruit Grassy
Smoky Coffee
Nutty Chocolate

💬 ADDITIONAL NOTES

_____
_____
_____
_____
_____
_____
_____
_____
_____
_____
_____
_____

🍷 PAIRED WITH

☆ SCORE

/5☆

WINE Tasting

NAME	
VARIETAL	VINTAGE
PRODUCER	ALCOHOL %
REGION	PRICE
TASTED AT	DATE

👁 APPEARANCE

Color Hue			Color Depth	Clarity	Viscosity
☐ Clear	☐ Pink	☐ Ruby	☐ Pale	☐ Clear	☐ Watery
☐ Straw	☐ Salmon	☐ Garnet	☐ Medium	☐ Hazy	☐ Medium
☐ Gold	☐ Orange	☐ Purple	☐ Deep	☐ Opaque	☐ Syrupy
☐ Brown	☐ Brick	☐			

AROMA

☐ Low ☐ Medium ☐ High Intensity

_____
_____
_____
_____
_____
_____
_____
_____

TASTE

☐ Sweet ☐ Tart ☐ Light
☐ Medium ☐ Fresh ☐ Medium
☐ Dry   ☐ Flabby ☐ Full-Bodied

_____
_____
_____
_____
_____
_____
_____

FINISH

☐ Short ☐ Medium ☐ Long

_____
_____
_____

😋 FLAVOR WHEEL

Leather   Mushroom
Mineral   Woody
Earthy   Herbal
Honey   Spicy
Dark Fruit   Floral
Tropical Fruit   Grassy
Smoky   Coffee
Nutty   Chocolate

💬 ADDITIONAL NOTES

_____
_____
_____
_____
_____
_____
_____
_____
_____
_____
_____
_____
_____
_____

🍷 PAIRED WITH

☆ SCORE

/5 ☆

WINE Tasting

NAME	
VARIETAL	VINTAGE
PRODUCER	ALCOHOL %
REGION	PRICE
TASTED AT	DATE

👁 APPEARANCE

Color Hue
☐ Clear ☐ Pink ☐ Ruby
☐ Straw ☐ Salmon ☐ Garnet
☐ Gold ☐ Orange ☐ Purple
☐ Brown ☐ Brick ☐

Color Depth
☐ Pale
☐ Medium
☐ Deep

Clarity
☐ Clear
☐ Hazy
☐ Opaque

Viscosity
☐ Watery
☐ Medium
☐ Syrupy

AROMA
☐ Low ☐ Medium ☐ High Intensity

_____
_____
_____
_____
_____
_____
_____
_____

😋 FLAVOR WHEEL

Leather   Mushroom
Mineral   Woody
Earthy   Herbal
Honey   Spicy
Dark Fruit   Floral
Tropical Fruit   Grassy
Smoky   Coffee
Nutty   Chocolate

TASTE
☐ Sweet ☐ Tart ☐ Light
☐ Medium ☐ Fresh ☐ Medium
☐ Dry ☐ Flabby ☐ Full-Bodied

_____
_____
_____
_____
_____
_____
_____
_____
_____
_____

💬 ADDITIONAL NOTES

_____
_____
_____
_____
_____
_____
_____
_____
_____
_____

FINISH
☐ Short ☐ Medium ☐ Long

_____
_____
_____

🍷 PAIRED WITH

⭐ SCORE

/5 ☆

50

WINE Tasting

NAME	
VARIETAL	VINTAGE
PRODUCER	ALCOHOL %
REGION	PRICE
TASTED AT	DATE

👁 APPEARANCE

Color Hue			Color Depth	Clarity	Viscosity
☐ Clear	☐ Pink	☐ Ruby	☐ Pale	☐ Clear	☐ Watery
☐ Straw	☐ Salmon	☐ Garnet	☐ Medium	☐ Hazy	☐ Medium
☐ Gold	☐ Orange	☐ Purple	☐ Deep	☐ Opaque	☐ Syrupy
☐ Brown	☐ Brick	☐			

AROMA

☐ Low ☐ Medium ☐ High Intensity

_____
_____
_____
_____
_____
_____
_____

TASTE

☐ Sweet ☐ Tart ☐ Light
☐ Medium ☐ Fresh ☐ Medium
☐ Dry ☐ Flabby ☐ Full-Bodied

_____
_____
_____
_____
_____
_____
_____
_____
_____

FINISH

☐ Short ☐ Medium ☐ Long

_____
_____
_____

😋 FLAVOR WHEEL

Leather   Mushroom
Mineral   Woody
Earthy   Herbal
Honey   Spicy
Dark Fruit   Floral
Tropical Fruit   Grassy
Smoky   Coffee
Nutty   Chocolate

💬 ADDITIONAL NOTES

_____
_____
_____
_____
_____
_____
_____
_____
_____
_____
_____

🍷 PAIRED WITH

☆ SCORE

/5 ☆

WINE Tasting

NAME	
VARIETAL	**VINTAGE**
PRODUCER	**ALCOHOL %**
REGION	**PRICE**
TASTED AT	**DATE**

👁 APPEARANCE

Color Hue
- ☐ Clear
- ☐ Straw
- ☐ Gold
- ☐ Brown
- ☐ Pink
- ☐ Salmon
- ☐ Orange
- ☐ Brick
- ☐ Ruby
- ☐ Garnet
- ☐ Purple

Color Depth
- ☐ Pale
- ☐ Medium
- ☐ Deep

Clarity
- ☐ Clear
- ☐ Hazy
- ☐ Opaque

Viscosity
- ☐ Watery
- ☐ Medium
- ☐ Syrupy

AROMA

☐ Low ☐ Medium ☐ High Intensity

_____
_____
_____
_____
_____
_____
_____

TASTE

- ☐ Sweet
- ☐ Medium
- ☐ Dry
- ☐ Tart
- ☐ Fresh
- ☐ Flabby
- ☐ Light
- ☐ Medium
- ☐ Full-Bodied

_____
_____
_____
_____
_____
_____
_____
_____

FINISH

☐ Short ☐ Medium ☐ Long

_____
_____

😋 FLAVOR WHEEL

Leather Mushroom
Mineral Woody
Earthy Herbal
Honey Spicy
Dark Fruit Floral
Tropical Fruit Grassy
Smoky Coffee
Nutty Chocolate

💬 ADDITIONAL NOTES

_____
_____
_____
_____
_____
_____
_____
_____
_____
_____
_____

🍷 PAIRED WITH

☆ SCORE

/5 ☆

52

WINE Tasting

NAME	
VARIETAL	VINTAGE
PRODUCER	ALCOHOL %
REGION	PRICE
TASTED AT	DATE

👁 APPEARANCE

Color Hue
- ☐ Clear
- ☐ Straw
- ☐ Gold
- ☐ Brown
- ☐ Pink
- ☐ Salmon
- ☐ Orange
- ☐ Brick
- ☐ Ruby
- ☐ Garnet
- ☐ Purple
- ☐

Color Depth
- ☐ Pale
- ☐ Medium
- ☐ Deep

Clarity
- ☐ Clear
- ☐ Hazy
- ☐ Opaque

Viscosity
- ☐ Watery
- ☐ Medium
- ☐ Syrupy

AROMA
☐ Low ☐ Medium ☐ High Intensity

_____
_____
_____
_____
_____
_____
_____
_____

😋 FLAVOR WHEEL

Leather Mushroom
Mineral Woody
Earthy Herbal
Honey Spicy
Dark Fruit Floral
Tropical Fruit Grassy
Smoky Coffee
Nutty Chocolate

TASTE
- ☐ Sweet
- ☐ Medium
- ☐ Dry
- ☐ Tart
- ☐ Fresh
- ☐ Flabby
- ☐ Light
- ☐ Medium
- ☐ Full-Bodied

_____
_____
_____
_____
_____
_____
_____
_____
_____
_____

💬 ADDITIONAL NOTES

_____
_____
_____
_____
_____
_____
_____
_____
_____

FINISH
☐ Short ☐ Medium ☐ Long

_____
_____
_____

🍷 PAIRED WITH

☆ SCORE

/5 ☆

WINE Tasting

NAME	
VARIETAL	**VINTAGE**
PRODUCER	**ALCOHOL %**
REGION	**PRICE**
TASTED AT	**DATE**

👁 APPEARANCE

Color Hue
- ☐ Clear
- ☐ Straw
- ☐ Gold
- ☐ Brown
- ☐ Pink
- ☐ Salmon
- ☐ Orange
- ☐ Brick
- ☐ Ruby
- ☐ Garnet
- ☐ Purple
- ☐

Color Depth
- ☐ Pale
- ☐ Medium
- ☐ Deep

Clarity
- ☐ Clear
- ☐ Hazy
- ☐ Opaque

Viscosity
- ☐ Watery
- ☐ Medium
- ☐ Syrupy

AROMA

☐ Low ☐ Medium ☐ High Intensity

_____
_____
_____
_____
_____
_____
_____

😋 FLAVOR WHEEL

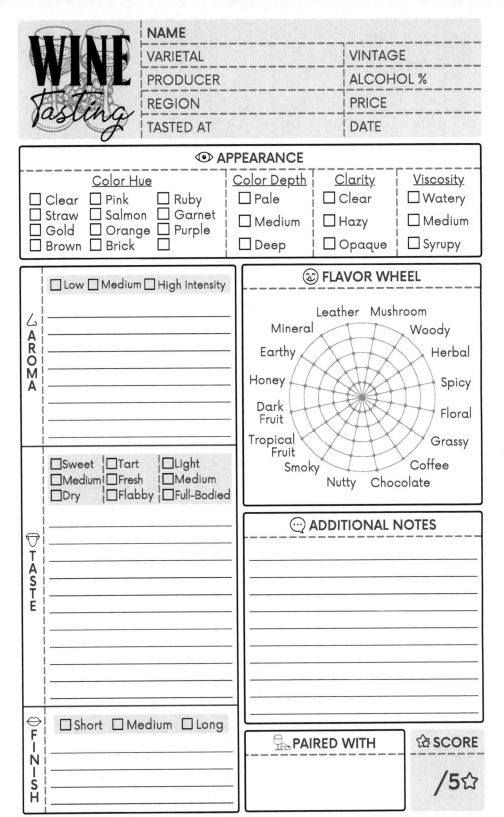

Leather   Mushroom
Mineral   Woody
Earthy   Herbal
Honey   Spicy
Dark Fruit   Floral
Tropical Fruit   Grassy
Smoky   Coffee
Nutty   Chocolate

TASTE

- ☐ Sweet
- ☐ Medium
- ☐ Dry
- ☐ Tart
- ☐ Fresh
- ☐ Flabby
- ☐ Light
- ☐ Medium
- ☐ Full-Bodied

_____
_____
_____
_____
_____
_____

💬 ADDITIONAL NOTES

_____
_____
_____
_____
_____
_____
_____
_____
_____
_____
_____

FINISH

☐ Short ☐ Medium ☐ Long

_____
_____
_____
_____

🍴 PAIRED WITH

☆ SCORE

/5 ☆

WINE Tasting

NAME	
VARIETAL	VINTAGE
PRODUCER	ALCOHOL %
REGION	PRICE
TASTED AT	DATE

👁 APPEARANCE

Color Hue
- ☐ Clear
- ☐ Straw
- ☐ Gold
- ☐ Brown
- ☐ Pink
- ☐ Salmon
- ☐ Orange
- ☐ Brick
- ☐ Ruby
- ☐ Garnet
- ☐ Purple
- ☐

Color Depth
- ☐ Pale
- ☐ Medium
- ☐ Deep

Clarity
- ☐ Clear
- ☐ Hazy
- ☐ Opaque

Viscosity
- ☐ Watery
- ☐ Medium
- ☐ Syrupy

AROMA

☐ Low ☐ Medium ☐ High Intensity

_____
_____
_____
_____
_____
_____
_____

😊 FLAVOR WHEEL

Leather   Mushroom
Mineral   Woody
Earthy   Herbal
Honey   Spicy
Dark Fruit   Floral
Tropical Fruit   Grassy
Smoky   Coffee
Nutty   Chocolate

TASTE

- ☐ Sweet
- ☐ Medium
- ☐ Dry
- ☐ Tart
- ☐ Fresh
- ☐ Flabby
- ☐ Light
- ☐ Medium
- ☐ Full-Bodied

_____
_____
_____
_____
_____
_____
_____
_____

💬 ADDITIONAL NOTES

_____
_____
_____
_____
_____
_____
_____
_____
_____

FINISH

☐ Short ☐ Medium ☐ Long

_____
_____
_____

🍷 PAIRED WITH

⭐ SCORE

/5 ☆

55

WINE Tasting

NAME	
VARIETAL	**VINTAGE**
PRODUCER	**ALCOHOL %**
REGION	**PRICE**
TASTED AT	**DATE**

👁 APPEARANCE

Color Hue
- ☐ Clear
- ☐ Straw
- ☐ Gold
- ☐ Brown
- ☐ Pink
- ☐ Salmon
- ☐ Orange
- ☐ Brick
- ☐ Ruby
- ☐ Garnet
- ☐ Purple
- ☐

Color Depth
- ☐ Pale
- ☐ Medium
- ☐ Deep

Clarity
- ☐ Clear
- ☐ Hazy
- ☐ Opaque

Viscosity
- ☐ Watery
- ☐ Medium
- ☐ Syrupy

AROMA
☐ Low ☐ Medium ☐ High Intensity

_____
_____
_____
_____
_____
_____

TASTE
- ☐ Sweet
- ☐ Medium
- ☐ Dry
- ☐ Tart
- ☐ Fresh
- ☐ Flabby
- ☐ Light
- ☐ Medium
- ☐ Full-Bodied

_____
_____
_____
_____
_____
_____

FINISH
☐ Short ☐ Medium ☐ Long

_____
_____
_____
_____

😋 FLAVOR WHEEL

Leather Mushroom
Mineral Woody
Earthy Herbal
Honey Spicy
Dark Fruit Floral
Tropical Fruit Grassy
Smoky Coffee
Nutty Chocolate

💬 ADDITIONAL NOTES

_____
_____
_____
_____
_____
_____
_____
_____
_____
_____
_____

🍷 PAIRED WITH

☆ SCORE

/5 ☆

WINE Tasting

NAME	
VARIETAL	VINTAGE
PRODUCER	ALCOHOL %
REGION	PRICE
TASTED AT	DATE

👁 APPEARANCE

Color Hue
☐ Clear ☐ Pink ☐ Ruby
☐ Straw ☐ Salmon ☐ Garnet
☐ Gold ☐ Orange ☐ Purple
☐ Brown ☐ Brick ☐

Color Depth
☐ Pale
☐ Medium
☐ Deep

Clarity
☐ Clear
☐ Hazy
☐ Opaque

Viscosity
☐ Watery
☐ Medium
☐ Syrupy

AROMA

☐ Low ☐ Medium ☐ High Intensity

_____
_____
_____
_____
_____
_____
_____

TASTE

☐ Sweet ☐ Tart ☐ Light
☐ Medium ☐ Fresh ☐ Medium
☐ Dry ☐ Flabby ☐ Full-Bodied

_____
_____
_____
_____
_____
_____
_____
_____
_____

FINISH

☐ Short ☐ Medium ☐ Long

_____
_____
_____

😋 FLAVOR WHEEL

Leather Mushroom
Mineral Woody
Earthy Herbal
Honey Spicy
Dark Fruit Floral
Tropical Fruit Grassy
Smoky Coffee
Nutty Chocolate

💬 ADDITIONAL NOTES

_____
_____
_____
_____
_____
_____
_____
_____
_____
_____

🍽 PAIRED WITH

☆ SCORE

/5 ☆

WINE Tasting

NAME	
VARIETAL	VINTAGE
PRODUCER	ALCOHOL %
REGION	PRICE
TASTED AT	DATE

👁 APPEARANCE

Color Hue
- ☐ Clear
- ☐ Straw
- ☐ Gold
- ☐ Brown
- ☐ Pink
- ☐ Salmon
- ☐ Orange
- ☐ Brick
- ☐ Ruby
- ☐ Garnet
- ☐ Purple
- ☐

Color Depth
- ☐ Pale
- ☐ Medium
- ☐ Deep

Clarity
- ☐ Clear
- ☐ Hazy
- ☐ Opaque

Viscosity
- ☐ Watery
- ☐ Medium
- ☐ Syrupy

AROMA

☐ Low ☐ Medium ☐ High Intensity

_____
_____
_____
_____
_____
_____
_____

😋 FLAVOR WHEEL

Leather Mushroom
Mineral Woody
Earthy Herbal
Honey Spicy
Dark Fruit Floral
Tropical Fruit Grassy
Smoky Coffee
Nutty Chocolate

TASTE

- ☐ Sweet
- ☐ Medium
- ☐ Dry
- ☐ Tart
- ☐ Fresh
- ☐ Flabby
- ☐ Light
- ☐ Medium
- ☐ Full-Bodied

_____
_____
_____
_____
_____
_____
_____
_____
_____
_____
_____

💬 ADDITIONAL NOTES

_____
_____
_____
_____
_____
_____
_____
_____
_____
_____
_____
_____

FINISH

☐ Short ☐ Medium ☐ Long

_____
_____
_____

🍷 PAIRED WITH

☆ SCORE

/5 ☆

WINE Tasting

NAME	
VARIETAL	VINTAGE
PRODUCER	ALCOHOL %
REGION	PRICE
TASTED AT	DATE

👁 APPEARANCE

Color Hue
- ☐ Clear
- ☐ Straw
- ☐ Gold
- ☐ Brown
- ☐ Pink
- ☐ Salmon
- ☐ Orange
- ☐ Brick
- ☐ Ruby
- ☐ Garnet
- ☐ Purple
- ☐

Color Depth
- ☐ Pale
- ☐ Medium
- ☐ Deep

Clarity
- ☐ Clear
- ☐ Hazy
- ☐ Opaque

Viscosity
- ☐ Watery
- ☐ Medium
- ☐ Syrupy

AROMA

☐ Low ☐ Medium ☐ High Intensity

_____
_____
_____
_____
_____
_____
_____

😋 FLAVOR WHEEL

Leather   Mushroom
Mineral   Woody
Earthy   Herbal
Honey   Spicy
Dark Fruit   Floral
Tropical Fruit   Grassy
Smoky   Coffee
Nutty   Chocolate

TASTE

- ☐ Sweet
- ☐ Medium
- ☐ Dry
- ☐ Tart
- ☐ Fresh
- ☐ Flabby
- ☐ Light
- ☐ Medium
- ☐ Full-Bodied

_____
_____
_____
_____
_____
_____
_____
_____
_____
_____

💬 ADDITIONAL NOTES

_____
_____
_____
_____
_____
_____
_____
_____
_____
_____

FINISH

☐ Short ☐ Medium ☐ Long

_____
_____
_____

🍷 PAIRED WITH

☆ SCORE

/5 ☆

WINE Tasting

NAME	
VARIETAL	**VINTAGE**
PRODUCER	**ALCOHOL %**
REGION	**PRICE**
TASTED AT	**DATE**

⊙ APPEARANCE

Color Hue
- ☐ Clear
- ☐ Straw
- ☐ Gold
- ☐ Brown
- ☐ Pink
- ☐ Salmon
- ☐ Orange
- ☐ Brick
- ☐ Ruby
- ☐ Garnet
- ☐ Purple

Color Depth
- ☐ Pale
- ☐ Medium
- ☐ Deep

Clarity
- ☐ Clear
- ☐ Hazy
- ☐ Opaque

Viscosity
- ☐ Watery
- ☐ Medium
- ☐ Syrupy

AROMA

☐ Low ☐ Medium ☐ High Intensity

_____
_____
_____
_____
_____
_____

☺ FLAVOR WHEEL

Leather Mushroom
Mineral Woody
Earthy Herbal
Honey Spicy
Dark Fruit Floral
Tropical Fruit Grassy
Smoky Coffee
Nutty Chocolate

TASTE

- ☐ Sweet
- ☐ Medium
- ☐ Dry
- ☐ Tart
- ☐ Fresh
- ☐ Flabby
- ☐ Light
- ☐ Medium
- ☐ Full-Bodied

_____
_____
_____
_____
_____
_____
_____
_____

☺ ADDITIONAL NOTES

_____
_____
_____
_____
_____
_____
_____
_____
_____
_____
_____
_____
_____

FINISH

☐ Short ☐ Medium ☐ Long

_____
_____
_____

🍷 PAIRED WITH

☆ SCORE

/5 ☆

WINE Tasting

NAME	
VARIETAL	VINTAGE
PRODUCER	ALCOHOL %
REGION	PRICE
TASTED AT	DATE

👁 APPEARANCE

Color Hue
- ☐ Clear
- ☐ Straw
- ☐ Gold
- ☐ Brown
- ☐ Pink
- ☐ Salmon
- ☐ Orange
- ☐ Brick
- ☐ Ruby
- ☐ Garnet
- ☐ Purple
- ☐

Color Depth
- ☐ Pale
- ☐ Medium
- ☐ Deep

Clarity
- ☐ Clear
- ☐ Hazy
- ☐ Opaque

Viscosity
- ☐ Watery
- ☐ Medium
- ☐ Syrupy

AROMA

☐ Low ☐ Medium ☐ High Intensity

_____
_____
_____
_____
_____
_____
_____

😋 FLAVOR WHEEL

Leather Mushroom
Mineral Woody
Earthy Herbal
Honey Spicy
Dark Fruit Floral
Tropical Fruit Grassy
Smoky Coffee
Nutty Chocolate

TASTE

- ☐ Sweet
- ☐ Medium
- ☐ Dry
- ☐ Tart
- ☐ Fresh
- ☐ Flabby
- ☐ Light
- ☐ Medium
- ☐ Full-Bodied

_____
_____
_____
_____
_____
_____
_____
_____
_____
_____

💬 ADDITIONAL NOTES

_____
_____
_____
_____
_____
_____
_____
_____
_____
_____
_____

FINISH

☐ Short ☐ Medium ☐ Long

_____
_____
_____
_____

🍷 PAIRED WITH

☆ SCORE

/5 ☆

WINE Tasting

NAME	
VARIETAL	VINTAGE
PRODUCER	ALCOHOL %
REGION	PRICE
TASTED AT	DATE

👁 APPEARANCE

Color Hue
- ☐ Clear
- ☐ Straw
- ☐ Gold
- ☐ Brown
- ☐ Pink
- ☐ Salmon
- ☐ Orange
- ☐ Brick
- ☐ Ruby
- ☐ Garnet
- ☐ Purple
- ☐

Color Depth
- ☐ Pale
- ☐ Medium
- ☐ Deep

Clarity
- ☐ Clear
- ☐ Hazy
- ☐ Opaque

Viscosity
- ☐ Watery
- ☐ Medium
- ☐ Syrupy

AROMA

☐ Low ☐ Medium ☐ High Intensity

_____
_____
_____
_____
_____
_____

TASTE

- ☐ Sweet
- ☐ Medium
- ☐ Dry
- ☐ Tart
- ☐ Fresh
- ☐ Flabby
- ☐ Light
- ☐ Medium
- ☐ Full-Bodied

_____
_____
_____
_____
_____
_____
_____
_____

FINISH

☐ Short ☐ Medium ☐ Long

_____
_____
_____

😋 FLAVOR WHEEL

Leather Mushroom
Mineral Woody
Earthy Herbal
Honey Spicy
Dark Fruit Floral
Tropical Fruit Grassy
Smoky Coffee
Nutty Chocolate

💬 ADDITIONAL NOTES

🍷 PAIRED WITH

☆ SCORE

/5 ☆

WINE Tasting

NAME	
VARIETAL	VINTAGE
PRODUCER	ALCOHOL %
REGION	PRICE
TASTED AT	DATE

👁 APPEARANCE

Color Hue
- ☐ Clear
- ☐ Straw
- ☐ Gold
- ☐ Brown
- ☐ Pink
- ☐ Salmon
- ☐ Orange
- ☐ Brick
- ☐ Ruby
- ☐ Garnet
- ☐ Purple
- ☐

Color Depth
- ☐ Pale
- ☐ Medium
- ☐ Deep

Clarity
- ☐ Clear
- ☐ Hazy
- ☐ Opaque

Viscosity
- ☐ Watery
- ☐ Medium
- ☐ Syrupy

AROMA
☐ Low ☐ Medium ☐ High Intensity

_____
_____
_____
_____
_____
_____
_____

TASTE
- ☐ Sweet
- ☐ Medium
- ☐ Dry
- ☐ Tart
- ☐ Fresh
- ☐ Flabby
- ☐ Light
- ☐ Medium
- ☐ Full-Bodied

_____
_____
_____
_____
_____
_____
_____
_____
_____
_____

FINISH
☐ Short ☐ Medium ☐ Long

_____
_____
_____

😋 FLAVOR WHEEL

Leather Mushroom
Mineral Woody
Earthy Herbal
Honey Spicy
Dark Fruit Floral
Tropical Fruit Grassy
Smoky Coffee
Nutty Chocolate

💬 ADDITIONAL NOTES

_____
_____
_____
_____
_____
_____
_____
_____
_____
_____
_____

🍷 PAIRED WITH

☆ SCORE

/5 ☆

63

WINE Tasting

NAME	
VARIETAL	VINTAGE
PRODUCER	ALCOHOL %
REGION	PRICE
TASTED AT	DATE

👁 APPEARANCE

Color Hue
- ☐ Clear
- ☐ Straw
- ☐ Gold
- ☐ Brown
- ☐ Pink
- ☐ Salmon
- ☐ Orange
- ☐ Brick
- ☐ Ruby
- ☐ Garnet
- ☐ Purple
- ☐

Color Depth
- ☐ Pale
- ☐ Medium
- ☐ Deep

Clarity
- ☐ Clear
- ☐ Hazy
- ☐ Opaque

Viscosity
- ☐ Watery
- ☐ Medium
- ☐ Syrupy

AROMA
☐ Low ☐ Medium ☐ High Intensity

_____
_____
_____
_____
_____
_____

TASTE
- ☐ Sweet
- ☐ Medium
- ☐ Dry
- ☐ Tart
- ☐ Fresh
- ☐ Flabby
- ☐ Light
- ☐ Medium
- ☐ Full-Bodied

_____
_____
_____
_____
_____
_____
_____
_____

FINISH
☐ Short ☐ Medium ☐ Long

_____
_____

😋 FLAVOR WHEEL

Leather Mushroom
Mineral   Woody
Earthy   Herbal
Honey   Spicy
Dark Fruit   Floral
Tropical Fruit   Grassy
Smoky   Coffee
Nutty Chocolate

💬 ADDITIONAL NOTES

_____
_____
_____
_____
_____
_____
_____
_____
_____
_____
_____

🍿 PAIRED WITH

☆ SCORE

/5 ☆

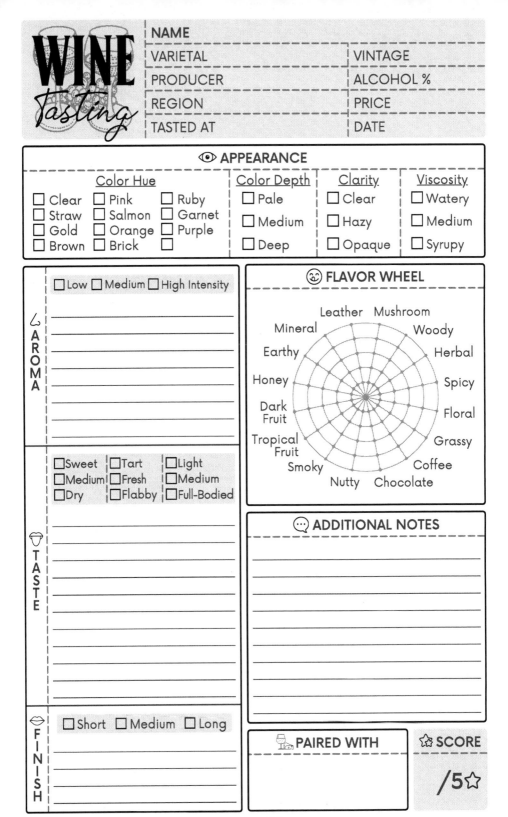

WINE Tasting

NAME	
VARIETAL	VINTAGE
PRODUCER	ALCOHOL %
REGION	PRICE
TASTED AT	DATE

👁 APPEARANCE

Color Hue
- ☐ Clear
- ☐ Straw
- ☐ Gold
- ☐ Brown
- ☐ Pink
- ☐ Salmon
- ☐ Orange
- ☐ Brick
- ☐ Ruby
- ☐ Garnet
- ☐ Purple
- ☐

Color Depth
- ☐ Pale
- ☐ Medium
- ☐ Deep

Clarity
- ☐ Clear
- ☐ Hazy
- ☐ Opaque

Viscosity
- ☐ Watery
- ☐ Medium
- ☐ Syrupy

AROMA

☐ Low ☐ Medium ☐ High Intensity

_____
_____
_____
_____
_____
_____
_____

TASTE

- ☐ Sweet
- ☐ Medium
- ☐ Dry
- ☐ Tart
- ☐ Fresh
- ☐ Flabby
- ☐ Light
- ☐ Medium
- ☐ Full-Bodied

_____
_____
_____
_____
_____
_____
_____
_____
_____
_____
_____

FINISH

☐ Short ☐ Medium ☐ Long

_____
_____
_____

😋 FLAVOR WHEEL

Leather Mushroom
Mineral   Woody
Earthy   Herbal
Honey   Spicy
Dark Fruit   Floral
Tropical Fruit   Grassy
Smoky   Coffee
Nutty Chocolate

💬 ADDITIONAL NOTES

_____
_____
_____
_____
_____
_____
_____
_____
_____
_____
_____
_____
_____

🍷 PAIRED WITH

⭐ SCORE

/5 ☆

WINE Tasting

NAME	
VARIETAL	VINTAGE
PRODUCER	ALCOHOL %
REGION	PRICE
TASTED AT	DATE

⊙ APPEARANCE

Color Hue
- ☐ Clear
- ☐ Straw
- ☐ Gold
- ☐ Brown
- ☐ Pink
- ☐ Salmon
- ☐ Orange
- ☐ Brick
- ☐ Ruby
- ☐ Garnet
- ☐ Purple

Color Depth
- ☐ Pale
- ☐ Medium
- ☐ Deep

Clarity
- ☐ Clear
- ☐ Hazy
- ☐ Opaque

Viscosity
- ☐ Watery
- ☐ Medium
- ☐ Syrupy

AROMA

☐ Low ☐ Medium ☐ High Intensity

_____
_____
_____
_____
_____
_____

☺ FLAVOR WHEEL

Leather Mushroom
Mineral Woody
Earthy Herbal
Honey Spicy
Dark Fruit Floral
Tropical Fruit Grassy
Smoky Coffee
Nutty Chocolate

TASTE

- ☐ Sweet
- ☐ Medium
- ☐ Dry
- ☐ Tart
- ☐ Fresh
- ☐ Flabby
- ☐ Light
- ☐ Medium
- ☐ Full-Bodied

_____
_____
_____
_____
_____
_____
_____
_____
_____
_____

☺ ADDITIONAL NOTES

_____
_____
_____
_____
_____
_____
_____
_____
_____
_____
_____

FINISH

☐ Short ☐ Medium ☐ Long

_____
_____
_____
_____

🍷 PAIRED WITH

☆ SCORE

/5☆

66

WINE Tasting

NAME	
VARIETAL	**VINTAGE**
PRODUCER	**ALCOHOL %**
REGION	**PRICE**
TASTED AT	**DATE**

👁 APPEARANCE

Color Hue			Color Depth	Clarity	Viscosity
☐ Clear	☐ Pink	☐ Ruby	☐ Pale	☐ Clear	☐ Watery
☐ Straw	☐ Salmon	☐ Garnet	☐ Medium	☐ Hazy	☐ Medium
☐ Gold	☐ Orange	☐ Purple	☐ Deep	☐ Opaque	☐ Syrupy
☐ Brown	☐ Brick	☐			

AROMA

☐ Low ☐ Medium ☐ High Intensity

_____
_____
_____
_____
_____
_____
_____

TASTE

☐ Sweet	☐ Tart	☐ Light
☐ Medium	☐ Fresh	☐ Medium
☐ Dry	☐ Flabby	☐ Full-Bodied

_____
_____
_____
_____
_____
_____
_____
_____
_____

FINISH

☐ Short ☐ Medium ☐ Long

_____
_____
_____

😋 FLAVOR WHEEL

Leather Mushroom
Mineral Woody
Earthy Herbal
Honey Spicy
Dark Fruit Floral
Tropical Fruit Grassy
Smoky Coffee
Nutty Chocolate

💬 ADDITIONAL NOTES

_____
_____
_____
_____
_____
_____
_____
_____
_____

🍷 PAIRED WITH

☆ SCORE

/5 ☆

WINE Tasting

NAME	
VARIETAL	VINTAGE
PRODUCER	ALCOHOL %
REGION	PRICE
TASTED AT	DATE

👁 APPEARANCE

Color Hue
- ☐ Clear
- ☐ Straw
- ☐ Gold
- ☐ Brown
- ☐ Pink
- ☐ Salmon
- ☐ Orange
- ☐ Brick
- ☐ Ruby
- ☐ Garnet
- ☐ Purple
- ☐

Color Depth
- ☐ Pale
- ☐ Medium
- ☐ Deep

Clarity
- ☐ Clear
- ☐ Hazy
- ☐ Opaque

Viscosity
- ☐ Watery
- ☐ Medium
- ☐ Syrupy

AROMA

☐ Low ☐ Medium ☐ High Intensity

_____
_____
_____
_____
_____
_____

TASTE

- ☐ Sweet
- ☐ Medium
- ☐ Dry
- ☐ Tart
- ☐ Fresh
- ☐ Flabby
- ☐ Light
- ☐ Medium
- ☐ Full-Bodied

_____
_____
_____
_____
_____
_____
_____
_____
_____

FINISH

☐ Short ☐ Medium ☐ Long

_____
_____
_____

😊 FLAVOR WHEEL

Leather Mushroom
Mineral Woody
Earthy Herbal
Honey Spicy
Dark Fruit Floral
Tropical Fruit Grassy
Smoky Coffee
Nutty Chocolate

💬 ADDITIONAL NOTES

_____
_____
_____
_____
_____
_____
_____
_____
_____
_____

🍷 PAIRED WITH

☆ SCORE

/5 ☆

WINE Tasting

NAME	
VARIETAL	VINTAGE
PRODUCER	ALCOHOL %
REGION	PRICE
TASTED AT	DATE

👁 APPEARANCE

Color Hue
- ☐ Clear
- ☐ Straw
- ☐ Gold
- ☐ Brown
- ☐ Pink
- ☐ Salmon
- ☐ Orange
- ☐ Brick
- ☐ Ruby
- ☐ Garnet
- ☐ Purple
- ☐

Color Depth
- ☐ Pale
- ☐ Medium
- ☐ Deep

Clarity
- ☐ Clear
- ☐ Hazy
- ☐ Opaque

Viscosity
- ☐ Watery
- ☐ Medium
- ☐ Syrupy

AROMA

☐ Low ☐ Medium ☐ High Intensity

_____
_____
_____
_____
_____
_____
_____

😋 FLAVOR WHEEL

Leather Mushroom
Mineral Woody
Earthy Herbal
Honey Spicy
Dark Fruit Floral
Tropical Fruit Grassy
Smoky Coffee
Nutty Chocolate

TASTE

- ☐ Sweet
- ☐ Medium
- ☐ Dry
- ☐ Tart
- ☐ Fresh
- ☐ Flabby
- ☐ Light
- ☐ Medium
- ☐ Full-Bodied

_____
_____
_____
_____
_____
_____
_____
_____
_____
_____

💬 ADDITIONAL NOTES

_____
_____
_____
_____
_____
_____
_____
_____
_____
_____
_____

FINISH

☐ Short ☐ Medium ☐ Long

_____
_____
_____

🍷 PAIRED WITH

☆ SCORE

/5☆

WINE Tasting

NAME	
VARIETAL	VINTAGE
PRODUCER	ALCOHOL %
REGION	PRICE
TASTED AT	DATE

👁 APPEARANCE

Color Hue
- ☐ Clear
- ☐ Straw
- ☐ Gold
- ☐ Brown
- ☐ Pink
- ☐ Salmon
- ☐ Orange
- ☐ Brick
- ☐ Ruby
- ☐ Garnet
- ☐ Purple
- ☐

Color Depth
- ☐ Pale
- ☐ Medium
- ☐ Deep

Clarity
- ☐ Clear
- ☐ Hazy
- ☐ Opaque

Viscosity
- ☐ Watery
- ☐ Medium
- ☐ Syrupy

AROMA

☐ Low ☐ Medium ☐ High Intensity

_____
_____
_____
_____
_____
_____
_____

TASTE

- ☐ Sweet
- ☐ Medium
- ☐ Dry
- ☐ Tart
- ☐ Fresh
- ☐ Flabby
- ☐ Light
- ☐ Medium
- ☐ Full-Bodied

_____
_____
_____
_____
_____
_____
_____
_____
_____
_____

FINISH

☐ Short ☐ Medium ☐ Long

_____
_____
_____

😋 FLAVOR WHEEL

Leather Mushroom
Mineral Woody
Earthy Herbal
Honey Spicy
Dark Fruit Floral
Tropical Fruit Grassy
Smoky Coffee
Nutty Chocolate

💬 ADDITIONAL NOTES

_____
_____
_____
_____
_____
_____
_____
_____
_____
_____
_____

🍷 PAIRED WITH

⭐ SCORE

/5 ☆

WINE Tasting

NAME	
VARIETAL	VINTAGE
PRODUCER	ALCOHOL %
REGION	PRICE
TASTED AT	DATE

👁 APPEARANCE

Color Hue
- ☐ Clear
- ☐ Straw
- ☐ Gold
- ☐ Brown
- ☐ Pink
- ☐ Salmon
- ☐ Orange
- ☐ Brick
- ☐ Ruby
- ☐ Garnet
- ☐ Purple
- ☐

Color Depth
- ☐ Pale
- ☐ Medium
- ☐ Deep

Clarity
- ☐ Clear
- ☐ Hazy
- ☐ Opaque

Viscosity
- ☐ Watery
- ☐ Medium
- ☐ Syrupy

AROMA

☐ Low ☐ Medium ☐ High Intensity

_____
_____
_____
_____
_____
_____

TASTE

☐ Sweet ☐ Tart ☐ Light
☐ Medium ☐ Fresh ☐ Medium
☐ Dry ☐ Flabby ☐ Full-Bodied

_____
_____
_____
_____
_____
_____
_____
_____
_____

FINISH

☐ Short ☐ Medium ☐ Long

_____
_____
_____

😋 FLAVOR WHEEL

Leather Mushroom
Mineral Woody
Earthy Herbal
Honey Spicy
Dark Fruit Floral
Tropical Fruit Grassy
Smoky Coffee
Nutty Chocolate

💬 ADDITIONAL NOTES

_____
_____
_____
_____
_____
_____
_____
_____
_____
_____
_____

🍽 PAIRED WITH

⭐ SCORE

/5 ☆

WINE Tasting

NAME	
VARIETAL	VINTAGE
PRODUCER	ALCOHOL %
REGION	PRICE
TASTED AT	DATE

👁 APPEARANCE

Color Hue
- ☐ Clear
- ☐ Straw
- ☐ Gold
- ☐ Brown
- ☐ Pink
- ☐ Salmon
- ☐ Orange
- ☐ Brick
- ☐ Ruby
- ☐ Garnet
- ☐ Purple
- ☐

Color Depth
- ☐ Pale
- ☐ Medium
- ☐ Deep

Clarity
- ☐ Clear
- ☐ Hazy
- ☐ Opaque

Viscosity
- ☐ Watery
- ☐ Medium
- ☐ Syrupy

AROMA

☐ Low ☐ Medium ☐ High Intensity

_____
_____
_____
_____
_____
_____
_____

TASTE

- ☐ Sweet
- ☐ Medium
- ☐ Dry
- ☐ Tart
- ☐ Fresh
- ☐ Flabby
- ☐ Light
- ☐ Medium
- ☐ Full-Bodied

_____
_____
_____
_____
_____
_____
_____
_____

FINISH

☐ Short ☐ Medium ☐ Long

_____
_____
_____
_____

😋 FLAVOR WHEEL

Leather Mushroom
Mineral Woody
Earthy Herbal
Honey Spicy
Dark Fruit Floral
Tropical Fruit Grassy
Smoky Coffee
Nutty Chocolate

💬 ADDITIONAL NOTES

_____
_____
_____
_____
_____
_____
_____
_____
_____
_____
_____

🍷 PAIRED WITH

☆ SCORE

/5 ☆

WINE Tasting

NAME	
VARIETAL	VINTAGE
PRODUCER	ALCOHOL %
REGION	PRICE
TASTED AT	DATE

◉ APPEARANCE

Color Hue
- ☐ Clear
- ☐ Straw
- ☐ Gold
- ☐ Brown
- ☐ Pink
- ☐ Salmon
- ☐ Orange
- ☐ Brick
- ☐ Ruby
- ☐ Garnet
- ☐ Purple
- ☐

Color Depth
- ☐ Pale
- ☐ Medium
- ☐ Deep

Clarity
- ☐ Clear
- ☐ Hazy
- ☐ Opaque

Viscosity
- ☐ Watery
- ☐ Medium
- ☐ Syrupy

AROMA

☐ Low ☐ Medium ☐ High Intensity

_____
_____
_____
_____
_____
_____
_____

TASTE

- ☐ Sweet
- ☐ Medium
- ☐ Dry
- ☐ Tart
- ☐ Fresh
- ☐ Flabby
- ☐ Light
- ☐ Medium
- ☐ Full-Bodied

_____
_____
_____
_____
_____
_____
_____
_____
_____
_____

FINISH

☐ Short ☐ Medium ☐ Long

_____
_____
_____

☺ FLAVOR WHEEL

Leather Mushroom
Mineral Woody
Earthy Herbal
Honey Spicy
Dark Fruit Floral
Tropical Fruit Grassy
Smoky Coffee
Nutty Chocolate

💬 ADDITIONAL NOTES

_____
_____
_____
_____
_____
_____
_____
_____
_____
_____

🍷 PAIRED WITH

☆ SCORE

/5 ☆

WINE Tasting

NAME	
VARIETAL	VINTAGE
PRODUCER	ALCOHOL %
REGION	PRICE
TASTED AT	DATE

👁 APPEARANCE

Color Hue			Color Depth	Clarity	Viscosity
☐ Clear	☐ Pink	☐ Ruby	☐ Pale	☐ Clear	☐ Watery
☐ Straw	☐ Salmon	☐ Garnet	☐ Medium	☐ Hazy	☐ Medium
☐ Gold	☐ Orange	☐ Purple	☐ Deep	☐ Opaque	☐ Syrupy
☐ Brown	☐ Brick	☐			

AROMA

☐ Low ☐ Medium ☐ High Intensity

_____
_____
_____
_____
_____
_____
_____
_____

😋 FLAVOR WHEEL

Leather Mushroom
Mineral Woody
Earthy Herbal
Honey Spicy
Dark Fruit Floral
Tropical Fruit Grassy
Smoky Coffee
Nutty Chocolate

TASTE

☐ Sweet	☐ Tart	☐ Light
☐ Medium	☐ Fresh	☐ Medium
☐ Dry	☐ Flabby	☐ Full-Bodied

_____
_____
_____
_____
_____
_____
_____
_____
_____
_____
_____

💬 ADDITIONAL NOTES

_____
_____
_____
_____
_____
_____
_____
_____
_____
_____
_____

FINISH

☐ Short ☐ Medium ☐ Long

_____
_____
_____

🍷 PAIRED WITH

☆ SCORE

/5 ☆

WINE Tasting

NAME	
VARIETAL	VINTAGE
PRODUCER	ALCOHOL %
REGION	PRICE
TASTED AT	DATE

👁 APPEARANCE

Color Hue
- ☐ Clear
- ☐ Straw
- ☐ Gold
- ☐ Brown
- ☐ Pink
- ☐ Salmon
- ☐ Orange
- ☐ Brick
- ☐ Ruby
- ☐ Garnet
- ☐ Purple
- ☐

Color Depth
- ☐ Pale
- ☐ Medium
- ☐ Deep

Clarity
- ☐ Clear
- ☐ Hazy
- ☐ Opaque

Viscosity
- ☐ Watery
- ☐ Medium
- ☐ Syrupy

AROMA
☐ Low ☐ Medium ☐ High Intensity

_____
_____
_____
_____
_____
_____
_____

TASTE
- ☐ Sweet
- ☐ Medium
- ☐ Dry
- ☐ Tart
- ☐ Fresh
- ☐ Flabby
- ☐ Light
- ☐ Medium
- ☐ Full-Bodied

_____
_____
_____
_____
_____
_____
_____
_____
_____

FINISH
☐ Short ☐ Medium ☐ Long

_____
_____
_____
_____

😋 FLAVOR WHEEL

Leather   Mushroom
Mineral   Woody
Earthy   Herbal
Honey   Spicy
Dark Fruit   Floral
Tropical Fruit   Grassy
Smoky   Coffee
Nutty   Chocolate

💬 ADDITIONAL NOTES

_____
_____
_____
_____
_____
_____
_____
_____
_____
_____

🍷 PAIRED WITH

☆ SCORE

/5 ☆

WINE
Tasting

NAME	
VARIETAL	VINTAGE
PRODUCER	ALCOHOL %
REGION	PRICE
TASTED AT	DATE

◉ APPEARANCE

Color Hue
☐ Clear ☐ Pink ☐ Ruby
☐ Straw ☐ Salmon ☐ Garnet
☐ Gold ☐ Orange ☐ Purple
☐ Brown ☐ Brick ☐

Color Depth
☐ Pale
☐ Medium
☐ Deep

Clarity
☐ Clear
☐ Hazy
☐ Opaque

Viscosity
☐ Watery
☐ Medium
☐ Syrupy

AROMA
☐ Low ☐ Medium ☐ High Intensity

_____
_____
_____
_____
_____
_____
_____

TASTE
☐ Sweet ☐ Tart ☐ Light
☐ Medium ☐ Fresh ☐ Medium
☐ Dry ☐ Flabby ☐ Full-Bodied

_____
_____
_____
_____
_____
_____
_____
_____

FINISH
☐ Short ☐ Medium ☐ Long

_____
_____
_____

☺ FLAVOR WHEEL

Leather Mushroom
Mineral Woody
Earthy Herbal
Honey Spicy
Dark Fruit Floral
Tropical Fruit Grassy
Smoky Coffee
Nutty Chocolate

💬 ADDITIONAL NOTES

_____
_____
_____
_____
_____
_____
_____
_____
_____
_____

🍷 PAIRED WITH

☆ SCORE

/5☆

WINE Tasting

NAME	
VARIETAL	VINTAGE
PRODUCER	ALCOHOL %
REGION	PRICE
TASTED AT	DATE

👁 APPEARANCE

Color Hue
- ☐ Clear
- ☐ Straw
- ☐ Gold
- ☐ Brown
- ☐ Pink
- ☐ Salmon
- ☐ Orange
- ☐ Brick
- ☐ Ruby
- ☐ Garnet
- ☐ Purple
- ☐

Color Depth
- ☐ Pale
- ☐ Medium
- ☐ Deep

Clarity
- ☐ Clear
- ☐ Hazy
- ☐ Opaque

Viscosity
- ☐ Watery
- ☐ Medium
- ☐ Syrupy

AROMA
☐ Low ☐ Medium ☐ High Intensity

_____
_____
_____
_____
_____
_____
_____

TASTE
- ☐ Sweet
- ☐ Medium
- ☐ Dry
- ☐ Tart
- ☐ Fresh
- ☐ Flabby
- ☐ Light
- ☐ Medium
- ☐ Full-Bodied

_____
_____
_____
_____
_____
_____
_____
_____
_____
_____
_____

FINISH
☐ Short ☐ Medium ☐ Long

_____
_____
_____

😊 FLAVOR WHEEL

Leather   Mushroom
Mineral   Woody
Earthy   Herbal
Honey   Spicy
Dark Fruit   Floral
Tropical Fruit   Grassy
Smoky   Coffee
Nutty   Chocolate

💬 ADDITIONAL NOTES

_____
_____
_____
_____
_____
_____
_____
_____
_____
_____
_____

🍽 PAIRED WITH

⭐ SCORE

/5 ☆

77

WINE Tasting

NAME	
VARIETAL	VINTAGE
PRODUCER	ALCOHOL %
REGION	PRICE
TASTED AT	DATE

👁 APPEARANCE

Color Hue
- ☐ Clear
- ☐ Straw
- ☐ Gold
- ☐ Brown
- ☐ Pink
- ☐ Salmon
- ☐ Orange
- ☐ Brick
- ☐ Ruby
- ☐ Garnet
- ☐ Purple

Color Depth
- ☐ Pale
- ☐ Medium
- ☐ Deep

Clarity
- ☐ Clear
- ☐ Hazy
- ☐ Opaque

Viscosity
- ☐ Watery
- ☐ Medium
- ☐ Syrupy

AROMA

☐ Low ☐ Medium ☐ High Intensity

_____
_____
_____
_____
_____
_____
_____

TASTE

- ☐ Sweet
- ☐ Medium
- ☐ Dry
- ☐ Tart
- ☐ Fresh
- ☐ Flabby
- ☐ Light
- ☐ Medium
- ☐ Full-Bodied

_____
_____
_____
_____
_____
_____
_____
_____
_____

FINISH

☐ Short ☐ Medium ☐ Long

_____
_____
_____

😋 FLAVOR WHEEL

Leather Mushroom
Mineral Woody
Earthy Herbal
Honey Spicy
Dark Fruit Floral
Tropical Fruit Grassy
Smoky Coffee
Nutty Chocolate

💬 ADDITIONAL NOTES

_____
_____
_____
_____
_____
_____
_____
_____
_____
_____

🍷 PAIRED WITH

☆ SCORE

/5☆

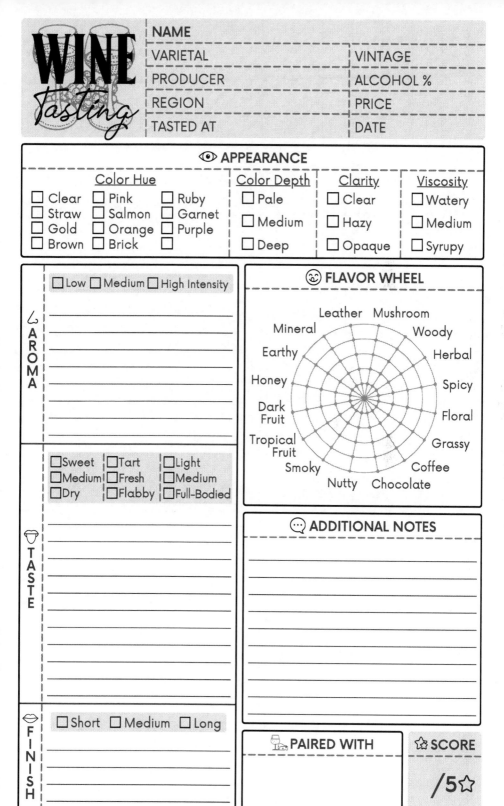

WINE Tasting

NAME	
VARIETAL	VINTAGE
PRODUCER	ALCOHOL %
REGION	PRICE
TASTED AT	DATE

👁 APPEARANCE

Color Hue
- ☐ Clear
- ☐ Straw
- ☐ Gold
- ☐ Brown
- ☐ Pink
- ☐ Salmon
- ☐ Orange
- ☐ Brick
- ☐ Ruby
- ☐ Garnet
- ☐ Purple
- ☐

Color Depth
- ☐ Pale
- ☐ Medium
- ☐ Deep

Clarity
- ☐ Clear
- ☐ Hazy
- ☐ Opaque

Viscosity
- ☐ Watery
- ☐ Medium
- ☐ Syrupy

AROMA

☐ Low ☐ Medium ☐ High Intensity

_____
_____
_____
_____
_____
_____

TASTE

- ☐ Sweet
- ☐ Medium
- ☐ Dry
- ☐ Tart
- ☐ Fresh
- ☐ Flabby
- ☐ Light
- ☐ Medium
- ☐ Full-Bodied

_____
_____
_____
_____
_____
_____
_____
_____
_____

FINISH

☐ Short ☐ Medium ☐ Long

_____
_____
_____

😋 FLAVOR WHEEL

Leather Mushroom
Mineral Woody
Earthy Herbal
Honey Spicy
Dark Fruit Floral
Tropical Fruit Grassy
Smoky Coffee
Nutty Chocolate

💬 ADDITIONAL NOTES

_____
_____
_____
_____
_____
_____
_____
_____
_____

🍽 PAIRED WITH

☆ SCORE

/5 ☆

WINE Tasting

NAME	
VARIETAL	VINTAGE
PRODUCER	ALCOHOL %
REGION	PRICE
TASTED AT	DATE

👁 APPEARANCE

Color Hue
- ☐ Clear
- ☐ Straw
- ☐ Gold
- ☐ Brown
- ☐ Pink
- ☐ Salmon
- ☐ Orange
- ☐ Brick
- ☐ Ruby
- ☐ Garnet
- ☐ Purple
- ☐

Color Depth
- ☐ Pale
- ☐ Medium
- ☐ Deep

Clarity
- ☐ Clear
- ☐ Hazy
- ☐ Opaque

Viscosity
- ☐ Watery
- ☐ Medium
- ☐ Syrupy

AROMA
☐ Low ☐ Medium ☐ High Intensity

_____
_____
_____
_____
_____
_____
_____

TASTE
- ☐ Sweet
- ☐ Medium
- ☐ Dry
- ☐ Tart
- ☐ Fresh
- ☐ Flabby
- ☐ Light
- ☐ Medium
- ☐ Full-Bodied

_____
_____
_____
_____
_____
_____
_____
_____

FINISH
☐ Short ☐ Medium ☐ Long

_____
_____
_____

😋 FLAVOR WHEEL

Leather Mushroom
Mineral Woody
Earthy Herbal
Honey Spicy
Dark Fruit Floral
Tropical Fruit Grassy
Smoky Coffee
Nutty Chocolate

💬 ADDITIONAL NOTES

_____
_____
_____
_____
_____
_____
_____
_____
_____
_____
_____
_____

🍷 PAIRED WITH

☆ SCORE

/5 ☆

WINE Tasting

NAME	
VARIETAL	VINTAGE
PRODUCER	ALCOHOL %
REGION	PRICE
TASTED AT	DATE

👁 APPEARANCE

Color Hue
- ☐ Clear
- ☐ Straw
- ☐ Gold
- ☐ Brown
- ☐ Pink
- ☐ Salmon
- ☐ Orange
- ☐ Brick
- ☐ Ruby
- ☐ Garnet
- ☐ Purple
- ☐

Color Depth
- ☐ Pale
- ☐ Medium
- ☐ Deep

Clarity
- ☐ Clear
- ☐ Hazy
- ☐ Opaque

Viscosity
- ☐ Watery
- ☐ Medium
- ☐ Syrupy

AROMA

☐ Low ☐ Medium ☐ High Intensity

_____
_____
_____
_____
_____
_____
_____

TASTE

- ☐ Sweet
- ☐ Medium
- ☐ Dry
- ☐ Tart
- ☐ Fresh
- ☐ Flabby
- ☐ Light
- ☐ Medium
- ☐ Full-Bodied

_____
_____
_____
_____
_____
_____
_____
_____
_____
_____

FINISH

☐ Short ☐ Medium ☐ Long

_____
_____
_____

😋 FLAVOR WHEEL

Leather   Mushroom
Mineral   Woody
Earthy   Herbal
Honey   Spicy
Dark Fruit   Floral
Tropical Fruit   Grassy
Smoky   Coffee
Nutty   Chocolate

💬 ADDITIONAL NOTES

_____
_____
_____
_____
_____
_____
_____
_____
_____
_____
_____

🍷 PAIRED WITH

☆ SCORE

/5 ☆

WINE Tasting

NAME	
VARIETAL	VINTAGE
PRODUCER	ALCOHOL %
REGION	PRICE
TASTED AT	DATE

👁 APPEARANCE

Color Hue
- ☐ Clear
- ☐ Straw
- ☐ Gold
- ☐ Brown
- ☐ Pink
- ☐ Salmon
- ☐ Orange
- ☐ Brick
- ☐ Ruby
- ☐ Garnet
- ☐ Purple
- ☐

Color Depth
- ☐ Pale
- ☐ Medium
- ☐ Deep

Clarity
- ☐ Clear
- ☐ Hazy
- ☐ Opaque

Viscosity
- ☐ Watery
- ☐ Medium
- ☐ Syrupy

AROMA

☐ Low ☐ Medium ☐ High Intensity

_____
_____
_____
_____
_____
_____
_____

TASTE

☐ Sweet ☐ Tart ☐ Light
☐ Medium ☐ Fresh ☐ Medium
☐ Dry ☐ Flabby ☐ Full-Bodied

_____
_____
_____
_____
_____
_____
_____
_____
_____

FINISH

☐ Short ☐ Medium ☐ Long

_____
_____
_____
_____

😋 FLAVOR WHEEL

Leather Mushroom
Mineral Woody
Earthy Herbal
Honey Spicy
Dark Fruit Floral
Tropical Fruit Grassy
Smoky Coffee
Nutty Chocolate

💬 ADDITIONAL NOTES

_____
_____
_____
_____
_____
_____
_____
_____
_____
_____
_____
_____

🍷 PAIRED WITH

☆ SCORE

/5 ☆

WINE Tasting

NAME	
VARIETAL	VINTAGE
PRODUCER	ALCOHOL %
REGION	PRICE
TASTED AT	DATE

◉ APPEARANCE

Color Hue
- ☐ Clear
- ☐ Straw
- ☐ Gold
- ☐ Brown
- ☐ Pink
- ☐ Salmon
- ☐ Orange
- ☐ Brick
- ☐ Ruby
- ☐ Garnet
- ☐ Purple
- ☐

Color Depth
- ☐ Pale
- ☐ Medium
- ☐ Deep

Clarity
- ☐ Clear
- ☐ Hazy
- ☐ Opaque

Viscosity
- ☐ Watery
- ☐ Medium
- ☐ Syrupy

AROMA

☐ Low ☐ Medium ☐ High Intensity

_____
_____
_____
_____
_____
_____

☺ FLAVOR WHEEL

Leather Mushroom
Mineral Woody
Earthy Herbal
Honey Spicy
Dark Fruit Floral
Tropical Fruit Grassy
Smoky Coffee
Nutty Chocolate

TASTE

- ☐ Sweet
- ☐ Medium
- ☐ Dry
- ☐ Tart
- ☐ Fresh
- ☐ Flabby
- ☐ Light
- ☐ Medium
- ☐ Full-Bodied

_____
_____
_____
_____
_____
_____
_____
_____
_____
_____
_____

💬 ADDITIONAL NOTES

_____
_____
_____
_____
_____
_____
_____
_____
_____
_____
_____
_____

FINISH

☐ Short ☐ Medium ☐ Long

_____
_____
_____

🍷 PAIRED WITH

☆ SCORE

/5 ☆

WINE
Tasting

NAME	
VARIETAL	VINTAGE
PRODUCER	ALCOHOL %
REGION	PRICE
TASTED AT	DATE

👁 APPEARANCE

Color Hue
- ☐ Clear
- ☐ Straw
- ☐ Gold
- ☐ Brown
- ☐ Pink
- ☐ Salmon
- ☐ Orange
- ☐ Brick
- ☐ Ruby
- ☐ Garnet
- ☐ Purple
- ☐

Color Depth
- ☐ Pale
- ☐ Medium
- ☐ Deep

Clarity
- ☐ Clear
- ☐ Hazy
- ☐ Opaque

Viscosity
- ☐ Watery
- ☐ Medium
- ☐ Syrupy

AROMA
☐ Low ☐ Medium ☐ High Intensity

_____
_____
_____
_____
_____
_____
_____

TASTE
- ☐ Sweet
- ☐ Medium
- ☐ Dry
- ☐ Tart
- ☐ Fresh
- ☐ Flabby
- ☐ Light
- ☐ Medium
- ☐ Full-Bodied

_____
_____
_____
_____
_____
_____
_____
_____

FINISH
☐ Short ☐ Medium ☐ Long

_____
_____
_____
_____

😋 FLAVOR WHEEL

Leather Mushroom
Mineral Woody
Earthy Herbal
Honey Spicy
Dark Fruit Floral
Tropical Fruit Grassy
Smoky Coffee
Nutty Chocolate

💬 ADDITIONAL NOTES

_____
_____
_____
_____
_____
_____
_____
_____
_____
_____
_____
_____

🍷 PAIRED WITH

☆ SCORE

/5 ☆

WINE Tasting

NAME	
VARIETAL	VINTAGE
PRODUCER	ALCOHOL %
REGION	PRICE
TASTED AT	DATE

👁 APPEARANCE

Color Hue			Color Depth	Clarity	Viscosity
☐ Clear	☐ Pink	☐ Ruby	☐ Pale	☐ Clear	☐ Watery
☐ Straw	☐ Salmon	☐ Garnet	☐ Medium	☐ Hazy	☐ Medium
☐ Gold	☐ Orange	☐ Purple	☐ Deep	☐ Opaque	☐ Syrupy
☐ Brown	☐ Brick	☐			

AROMA

☐ Low ☐ Medium ☐ High Intensity

_____
_____
_____
_____
_____
_____
_____

😋 FLAVOR WHEEL

Leather   Mushroom
Mineral   Woody
Earthy   Herbal
Honey   Spicy
Dark Fruit   Floral
Tropical Fruit   Grassy
Smoky   Coffee
Nutty   Chocolate

TASTE

☐ Sweet ☐ Tart ☐ Light
☐ Medium ☐ Fresh ☐ Medium
☐ Dry ☐ Flabby ☐ Full-Bodied

_____
_____
_____
_____
_____
_____
_____
_____
_____
_____

💬 ADDITIONAL NOTES

_____
_____
_____
_____
_____
_____
_____
_____
_____
_____
_____

FINISH

☐ Short ☐ Medium ☐ Long

_____
_____
_____

🍽 PAIRED WITH

☆ SCORE

/5 ☆

WINE Tasting

NAME	
VARIETAL	VINTAGE
PRODUCER	ALCOHOL %
REGION	PRICE
TASTED AT	DATE

👁 APPEARANCE

Color Hue
- ☐ Clear
- ☐ Straw
- ☐ Gold
- ☐ Brown
- ☐ Pink
- ☐ Salmon
- ☐ Orange
- ☐ Brick
- ☐ Ruby
- ☐ Garnet
- ☐ Purple
- ☐

Color Depth
- ☐ Pale
- ☐ Medium
- ☐ Deep

Clarity
- ☐ Clear
- ☐ Hazy
- ☐ Opaque

Viscosity
- ☐ Watery
- ☐ Medium
- ☐ Syrupy

AROMA
☐ Low ☐ Medium ☐ High Intensity

_____
_____
_____
_____
_____
_____

TASTE
- ☐ Sweet
- ☐ Medium
- ☐ Dry
- ☐ Tart
- ☐ Fresh
- ☐ Flabby
- ☐ Light
- ☐ Medium
- ☐ Full-Bodied

_____
_____
_____
_____
_____
_____
_____
_____
_____

FINISH
☐ Short ☐ Medium ☐ Long

_____
_____
_____

😋 FLAVOR WHEEL

Leather Mushroom
Mineral Woody
Earthy Herbal
Honey Spicy
Dark Fruit Floral
Tropical Fruit Grassy
Smoky Coffee
Nutty Chocolate

💬 ADDITIONAL NOTES

_____
_____
_____
_____
_____
_____
_____
_____
_____
_____
_____

🍽 PAIRED WITH

☆ SCORE

/5 ☆

WINE Tasting

NAME	
VARIETAL	VINTAGE
PRODUCER	ALCOHOL %
REGION	PRICE
TASTED AT	DATE

👁 APPEARANCE

Color Hue
- ☐ Clear
- ☐ Straw
- ☐ Gold
- ☐ Brown
- ☐ Pink
- ☐ Salmon
- ☐ Orange
- ☐ Brick
- ☐ Ruby
- ☐ Garnet
- ☐ Purple
- ☐

Color Depth
- ☐ Pale
- ☐ Medium
- ☐ Deep

Clarity
- ☐ Clear
- ☐ Hazy
- ☐ Opaque

Viscosity
- ☐ Watery
- ☐ Medium
- ☐ Syrupy

AROMA
☐ Low ☐ Medium ☐ High Intensity

_____
_____
_____
_____
_____
_____
_____

😋 FLAVOR WHEEL

Leather Mushroom
Mineral Woody
Earthy Herbal
Honey Spicy
Dark Fruit Floral
Tropical Fruit Grassy
Smoky Coffee
Nutty Chocolate

TASTE
- ☐ Sweet
- ☐ Medium
- ☐ Dry
- ☐ Tart
- ☐ Fresh
- ☐ Flabby
- ☐ Light
- ☐ Medium
- ☐ Full-Bodied

_____
_____
_____
_____
_____
_____
_____
_____
_____
_____
_____

💬 ADDITIONAL NOTES

_____
_____
_____
_____
_____
_____
_____
_____
_____

FINISH
☐ Short ☐ Medium ☐ Long

_____
_____
_____
_____

🍷 PAIRED WITH

☆ SCORE
/5 ☆

87

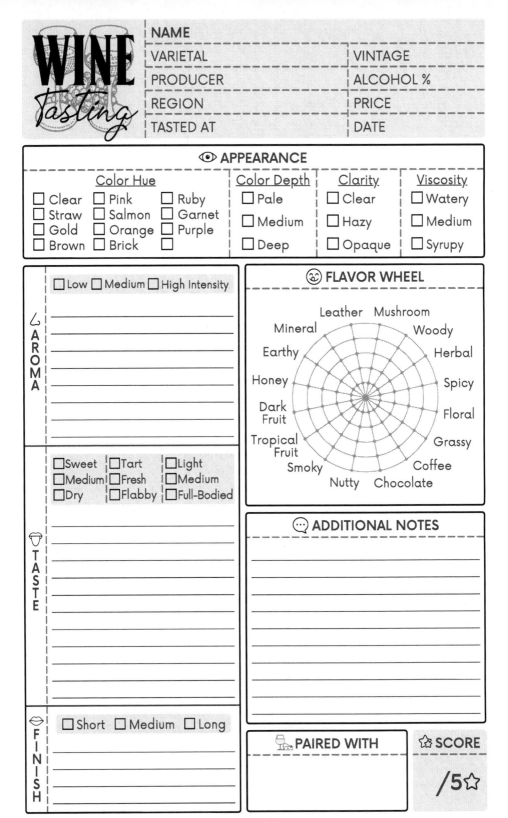

WINE Tasting

NAME	
VARIETAL	VINTAGE
PRODUCER	ALCOHOL %
REGION	PRICE
TASTED AT	DATE

👁 APPEARANCE

Color Hue
- ☐ Clear
- ☐ Straw
- ☐ Gold
- ☐ Brown
- ☐ Pink
- ☐ Salmon
- ☐ Orange
- ☐ Brick
- ☐ Ruby
- ☐ Garnet
- ☐ Purple
- ☐

Color Depth
- ☐ Pale
- ☐ Medium
- ☐ Deep

Clarity
- ☐ Clear
- ☐ Hazy
- ☐ Opaque

Viscosity
- ☐ Watery
- ☐ Medium
- ☐ Syrupy

AROMA
☐ Low ☐ Medium ☐ High Intensity

_____
_____
_____
_____
_____
_____
_____

TASTE
- ☐ Sweet
- ☐ Medium
- ☐ Dry
- ☐ Tart
- ☐ Fresh
- ☐ Flabby
- ☐ Light
- ☐ Medium
- ☐ Full-Bodied

_____
_____
_____
_____
_____
_____
_____
_____
_____
_____

FINISH
☐ Short ☐ Medium ☐ Long

_____
_____
_____

😋 FLAVOR WHEEL

Leather Mushroom
Mineral Woody
Earthy Herbal
Honey Spicy
Dark Fruit Floral
Tropical Fruit Grassy
Smoky Coffee
Nutty Chocolate

💬 ADDITIONAL NOTES

_____
_____
_____
_____
_____
_____
_____
_____
_____
_____
_____
_____
_____

🍷 PAIRED WITH

☆ SCORE

/5 ☆

WINE Tasting

NAME	
VARIETAL	VINTAGE
PRODUCER	ALCOHOL %
REGION	PRICE
TASTED AT	DATE

👁 APPEARANCE

Color Hue
☐ Clear ☐ Pink ☐ Ruby
☐ Straw ☐ Salmon ☐ Garnet
☐ Gold ☐ Orange ☐ Purple
☐ Brown ☐ Brick ☐

Color Depth
☐ Pale
☐ Medium
☐ Deep

Clarity
☐ Clear
☐ Hazy
☐ Opaque

Viscosity
☐ Watery
☐ Medium
☐ Syrupy

AROMA

☐ Low ☐ Medium ☐ High Intensity

_____
_____
_____
_____
_____
_____
_____

😋 FLAVOR WHEEL

Leather Mushroom
Mineral Woody
Earthy Herbal
Honey Spicy
Dark Fruit Floral
Tropical Fruit Grassy
Smoky Coffee
Nutty Chocolate

TASTE

☐ Sweet ☐ Tart ☐ Light
☐ Medium ☐ Fresh ☐ Medium
☐ Dry ☐ Flabby ☐ Full-Bodied

_____
_____
_____
_____
_____
_____
_____
_____
_____
_____

💬 ADDITIONAL NOTES

_____
_____
_____
_____
_____
_____
_____
_____
_____
_____

FINISH

☐ Short ☐ Medium ☐ Long

_____
_____
_____

🍽 PAIRED WITH

☆ SCORE

/5 ☆

WINE Tasting

NAME	
VARIETAL	VINTAGE
PRODUCER	ALCOHOL %
REGION	PRICE
TASTED AT	DATE

👁 APPEARANCE

Color Hue
- ☐ Clear
- ☐ Straw
- ☐ Gold
- ☐ Brown
- ☐ Pink
- ☐ Salmon
- ☐ Orange
- ☐ Brick
- ☐ Ruby
- ☐ Garnet
- ☐ Purple
- ☐

Color Depth
- ☐ Pale
- ☐ Medium
- ☐ Deep

Clarity
- ☐ Clear
- ☐ Hazy
- ☐ Opaque

Viscosity
- ☐ Watery
- ☐ Medium
- ☐ Syrupy

AROMA
☐ Low ☐ Medium ☐ High Intensity

_____
_____
_____
_____
_____
_____

TASTE
- ☐ Sweet
- ☐ Medium
- ☐ Dry
- ☐ Tart
- ☐ Fresh
- ☐ Flabby
- ☐ Light
- ☐ Medium
- ☐ Full-Bodied

_____
_____
_____
_____
_____
_____
_____
_____
_____

FINISH
☐ Short ☐ Medium ☐ Long

_____
_____
_____

😋 FLAVOR WHEEL

Leather Mushroom
Mineral   Woody
Earthy   Herbal
Honey   Spicy
Dark
Fruit   Floral
Tropical
Fruit   Grassy
Smoky   Coffee
Nutty Chocolate

💬 ADDITIONAL NOTES

_____
_____
_____
_____
_____
_____
_____
_____
_____
_____
_____
_____

🍷 PAIRED WITH

☆ SCORE

/5☆

WINE Tasting

NAME	
VARIETAL	VINTAGE
PRODUCER	ALCOHOL %
REGION	PRICE
TASTED AT	DATE

👁 APPEARANCE

Color Hue
- ☐ Clear
- ☐ Straw
- ☐ Gold
- ☐ Brown
- ☐ Pink
- ☐ Salmon
- ☐ Orange
- ☐ Brick
- ☐ Ruby
- ☐ Garnet
- ☐ Purple
- ☐

Color Depth
- ☐ Pale
- ☐ Medium
- ☐ Deep

Clarity
- ☐ Clear
- ☐ Hazy
- ☐ Opaque

Viscosity
- ☐ Watery
- ☐ Medium
- ☐ Syrupy

AROMA

☐ Low ☐ Medium ☐ High Intensity

_____
_____
_____
_____
_____
_____
_____

TASTE

- ☐ Sweet
- ☐ Medium
- ☐ Dry
- ☐ Tart
- ☐ Fresh
- ☐ Flabby
- ☐ Light
- ☐ Medium
- ☐ Full-Bodied

_____
_____
_____
_____
_____
_____
_____
_____
_____
_____

FINISH

☐ Short ☐ Medium ☐ Long

_____
_____
_____

😋 FLAVOR WHEEL

Leather Mushroom
Mineral Woody
Earthy Herbal
Honey Spicy
Dark Fruit Floral
Tropical Fruit Grassy
Smoky Coffee
Nutty Chocolate

💬 ADDITIONAL NOTES

_____
_____
_____
_____
_____
_____
_____
_____
_____
_____
_____

🍷 PAIRED WITH

☆ SCORE

/5 ☆

WINE Tasting

NAME	
VARIETAL	VINTAGE
PRODUCER	ALCOHOL %
REGION	PRICE
TASTED AT	DATE

👁 APPEARANCE

Color Hue
- ☐ Clear
- ☐ Straw
- ☐ Gold
- ☐ Brown
- ☐ Pink
- ☐ Salmon
- ☐ Orange
- ☐ Brick
- ☐ Ruby
- ☐ Garnet
- ☐ Purple

Color Depth
- ☐ Pale
- ☐ Medium
- ☐ Deep

Clarity
- ☐ Clear
- ☐ Hazy
- ☐ Opaque

Viscosity
- ☐ Watery
- ☐ Medium
- ☐ Syrupy

AROMA
☐ Low ☐ Medium ☐ High Intensity

_____
_____
_____
_____
_____
_____
_____

TASTE
- ☐ Sweet
- ☐ Medium
- ☐ Dry
- ☐ Tart
- ☐ Fresh
- ☐ Flabby
- ☐ Light
- ☐ Medium
- ☐ Full-Bodied

_____
_____
_____
_____
_____
_____

FINISH
☐ Short ☐ Medium ☐ Long

_____

😋 FLAVOR WHEEL

Leather Mushroom
Mineral Woody
Earthy Herbal
Honey Spicy
Dark Fruit Floral
Tropical Fruit Grassy
Smoky Coffee
Nutty Chocolate

💬 ADDITIONAL NOTES

_____
_____
_____
_____
_____
_____
_____
_____
_____
_____
_____

🍷 PAIRED WITH

☆ SCORE

/5 ☆

92

WINE Tasting

NAME	
VARIETAL	VINTAGE
PRODUCER	ALCOHOL %
REGION	PRICE
TASTED AT	DATE

👁 APPEARANCE

Color Hue
- ☐ Clear
- ☐ Straw
- ☐ Gold
- ☐ Brown
- ☐ Pink
- ☐ Salmon
- ☐ Orange
- ☐ Brick
- ☐ Ruby
- ☐ Garnet
- ☐ Purple
- ☐

Color Depth
- ☐ Pale
- ☐ Medium
- ☐ Deep

Clarity
- ☐ Clear
- ☐ Hazy
- ☐ Opaque

Viscosity
- ☐ Watery
- ☐ Medium
- ☐ Syrupy

AROMA
☐ Low ☐ Medium ☐ High Intensity

_____
_____
_____
_____
_____
_____
_____

TASTE
- ☐ Sweet
- ☐ Medium
- ☐ Dry
- ☐ Tart
- ☐ Fresh
- ☐ Flabby
- ☐ Light
- ☐ Medium
- ☐ Full-Bodied

_____
_____
_____
_____
_____
_____
_____
_____
_____

FINISH
☐ Short ☐ Medium ☐ Long

_____
_____
_____

😊 FLAVOR WHEEL

Leather Mushroom
Mineral Woody
Earthy Herbal
Honey Spicy
Dark Fruit Floral
Tropical Fruit Grassy
Smoky Coffee
Nutty Chocolate

💬 ADDITIONAL NOTES

_____
_____
_____
_____
_____
_____
_____
_____
_____
_____
_____
_____

🍽 PAIRED WITH

☆ SCORE

/5 ☆

93

WINE Tasting

NAME	
VARIETAL	VINTAGE
PRODUCER	ALCOHOL %
REGION	PRICE
TASTED AT	DATE

👁 APPEARANCE

Color Hue
- ☐ Clear
- ☐ Straw
- ☐ Gold
- ☐ Brown
- ☐ Pink
- ☐ Salmon
- ☐ Orange
- ☐ Brick
- ☐ Ruby
- ☐ Garnet
- ☐ Purple
- ☐

Color Depth
- ☐ Pale
- ☐ Medium
- ☐ Deep

Clarity
- ☐ Clear
- ☐ Hazy
- ☐ Opaque

Viscosity
- ☐ Watery
- ☐ Medium
- ☐ Syrupy

AROMA

☐ Low ☐ Medium ☐ High Intensity

_____
_____
_____
_____
_____
_____
_____

TASTE

- ☐ Sweet
- ☐ Medium
- ☐ Dry
- ☐ Tart
- ☐ Fresh
- ☐ Flabby
- ☐ Light
- ☐ Medium
- ☐ Full-Bodied

_____
_____
_____
_____
_____
_____
_____
_____
_____

FINISH

☐ Short ☐ Medium ☐ Long

_____
_____
_____

😋 FLAVOR WHEEL

Leather Mushroom
Mineral Woody
Earthy Herbal
Honey Spicy
Dark Fruit Floral
Tropical Fruit Grassy
Smoky Coffee
Nutty Chocolate

💬 ADDITIONAL NOTES

_____
_____
_____
_____
_____
_____
_____
_____
_____
_____
_____
_____
_____

🍷 PAIRED WITH

⭐ SCORE

/5 ☆

WINE Tasting

NAME	
VARIETAL	VINTAGE
PRODUCER	ALCOHOL %
REGION	PRICE
TASTED AT	DATE

👁 APPEARANCE

Color Hue
- ☐ Clear
- ☐ Straw
- ☐ Gold
- ☐ Brown
- ☐ Pink
- ☐ Salmon
- ☐ Orange
- ☐ Brick
- ☐ Ruby
- ☐ Garnet
- ☐ Purple
- ☐

Color Depth
- ☐ Pale
- ☐ Medium
- ☐ Deep

Clarity
- ☐ Clear
- ☐ Hazy
- ☐ Opaque

Viscosity
- ☐ Watery
- ☐ Medium
- ☐ Syrupy

AROMA
☐ Low ☐ Medium ☐ High Intensity

TASTE
- ☐ Sweet
- ☐ Medium
- ☐ Dry
- ☐ Tart
- ☐ Fresh
- ☐ Flabby
- ☐ Light
- ☐ Medium
- ☐ Full-Bodied

FINISH
☐ Short ☐ Medium ☐ Long

😋 FLAVOR WHEEL

Leather Mushroom
Mineral Woody
Earthy Herbal
Honey Spicy
Dark Fruit Floral
Tropical Fruit Grassy
Smoky Coffee
Nutty Chocolate

💬 ADDITIONAL NOTES

🍴 PAIRED WITH

☆ SCORE

/5 ☆

95

WINE Tasting

NAME	
VARIETAL	VINTAGE
PRODUCER	ALCOHOL %
REGION	PRICE
TASTED AT	DATE

👁 APPEARANCE

Color Hue
- ☐ Clear
- ☐ Straw
- ☐ Gold
- ☐ Brown
- ☐ Pink
- ☐ Salmon
- ☐ Orange
- ☐ Brick
- ☐ Ruby
- ☐ Garnet
- ☐ Purple

Color Depth
- ☐ Pale
- ☐ Medium
- ☐ Deep

Clarity
- ☐ Clear
- ☐ Hazy
- ☐ Opaque

Viscosity
- ☐ Watery
- ☐ Medium
- ☐ Syrupy

AROMA
☐ Low ☐ Medium ☐ High Intensity

_____
_____
_____
_____
_____
_____

TASTE
- ☐ Sweet
- ☐ Medium
- ☐ Dry
- ☐ Tart
- ☐ Fresh
- ☐ Flabby
- ☐ Light
- ☐ Medium
- ☐ Full-Bodied

_____
_____
_____
_____
_____
_____

FINISH
☐ Short ☐ Medium ☐ Long

_____
_____

😊 FLAVOR WHEEL

Leather Mushroom
Mineral Woody
Earthy Herbal
Honey Spicy
Dark Fruit Floral
Tropical Fruit Grassy
Smoky Coffee
Nutty Chocolate

💬 ADDITIONAL NOTES

_____
_____
_____
_____
_____
_____
_____
_____
_____
_____
_____

🍷 PAIRED WITH

☆ SCORE

/5☆

WINE Tasting

NAME	
VARIETAL	VINTAGE
PRODUCER	ALCOHOL %
REGION	PRICE
TASTED AT	DATE

👁 APPEARANCE

Color Hue
- ☐ Clear
- ☐ Straw
- ☐ Gold
- ☐ Brown
- ☐ Pink
- ☐ Salmon
- ☐ Orange
- ☐ Brick
- ☐ Ruby
- ☐ Garnet
- ☐ Purple
- ☐

Color Depth
- ☐ Pale
- ☐ Medium
- ☐ Deep

Clarity
- ☐ Clear
- ☐ Hazy
- ☐ Opaque

Viscosity
- ☐ Watery
- ☐ Medium
- ☐ Syrupy

AROMA

☐ Low ☐ Medium ☐ High Intensity

_____
_____
_____
_____
_____
_____
_____

TASTE

- ☐ Sweet
- ☐ Medium
- ☐ Dry
- ☐ Tart
- ☐ Fresh
- ☐ Flabby
- ☐ Light
- ☐ Medium
- ☐ Full-Bodied

_____
_____
_____
_____
_____
_____
_____
_____
_____
_____

FINISH

☐ Short ☐ Medium ☐ Long

_____
_____
_____

😋 FLAVOR WHEEL

Leather Mushroom
Mineral Woody
Earthy Herbal
Honey Spicy
Dark Fruit Floral
Tropical Fruit Grassy
Smoky Coffee
Nutty Chocolate

💬 ADDITIONAL NOTES

_____
_____
_____
_____
_____
_____
_____
_____
_____
_____
_____

🍽 PAIRED WITH

☆ SCORE

/5☆

WINE Tasting

NAME	
VARIETAL	VINTAGE
PRODUCER	ALCOHOL %
REGION	PRICE
TASTED AT	DATE

👁 APPEARANCE

Color Hue
- ☐ Clear
- ☐ Straw
- ☐ Gold
- ☐ Brown
- ☐ Pink
- ☐ Salmon
- ☐ Orange
- ☐ Brick
- ☐ Ruby
- ☐ Garnet
- ☐ Purple

Color Depth
- ☐ Pale
- ☐ Medium
- ☐ Deep

Clarity
- ☐ Clear
- ☐ Hazy
- ☐ Opaque

Viscosity
- ☐ Watery
- ☐ Medium
- ☐ Syrupy

AROMA
☐ Low ☐ Medium ☐ High Intensity

_____
_____
_____
_____
_____
_____

TASTE
- ☐ Sweet
- ☐ Medium
- ☐ Dry
- ☐ Tart
- ☐ Fresh
- ☐ Flabby
- ☐ Light
- ☐ Medium
- ☐ Full-Bodied

_____
_____
_____
_____
_____
_____
_____
_____
_____

FINISH
☐ Short ☐ Medium ☐ Long

_____
_____
_____
_____

😋 FLAVOR WHEEL

Leather Mushroom
Mineral Woody
Earthy Herbal
Honey Spicy
Dark Fruit Floral
Tropical Fruit Grassy
Smoky Coffee
Nutty Chocolate

💬 ADDITIONAL NOTES

_____
_____
_____
_____
_____
_____
_____
_____
_____
_____
_____
_____
_____

🍷 PAIRED WITH

☆ SCORE

/5 ☆

WINE Tasting

NAME	
VARIETAL	VINTAGE
PRODUCER	ALCOHOL %
REGION	PRICE
TASTED AT	DATE

👁 APPEARANCE

Color Hue			Color Depth	Clarity	Viscosity
☐ Clear	☐ Pink	☐ Ruby	☐ Pale	☐ Clear	☐ Watery
☐ Straw	☐ Salmon	☐ Garnet	☐ Medium	☐ Hazy	☐ Medium
☐ Gold	☐ Orange	☐ Purple	☐ Deep	☐ Opaque	☐ Syrupy
☐ Brown	☐ Brick	☐			

AROMA

☐ Low ☐ Medium ☐ High Intensity

_____
_____
_____
_____
_____
_____

TASTE

☐ Sweet ☐ Tart ☐ Light
☐ Medium ☐ Fresh ☐ Medium
☐ Dry ☐ Flabby ☐ Full-Bodied

_____
_____
_____
_____
_____
_____
_____
_____
_____
_____

FINISH

☐ Short ☐ Medium ☐ Long

_____
_____
_____

😋 FLAVOR WHEEL

Leather Mushroom
Mineral Woody
Earthy Herbal
Honey Spicy
Dark Fruit Floral
Tropical Fruit Grassy
Smoky Coffee
Nutty Chocolate

💬 ADDITIONAL NOTES

_____
_____
_____
_____
_____
_____
_____
_____
_____
_____

🍽 PAIRED WITH

☆ SCORE

/5 ☆

WINE *Tasting*

NAME	
VARIETAL	VINTAGE
PRODUCER	ALCOHOL %
REGION	PRICE
TASTED AT	DATE

👁 APPEARANCE

Color Hue			Color Depth	Clarity	Viscosity
☐ Clear	☐ Pink	☐ Ruby	☐ Pale	☐ Clear	☐ Watery
☐ Straw	☐ Salmon	☐ Garnet	☐ Medium	☐ Hazy	☐ Medium
☐ Gold	☐ Orange	☐ Purple	☐ Deep	☐ Opaque	☐ Syrupy
☐ Brown	☐ Brick	☐			

AROMA

☐ Low ☐ Medium ☐ High Intensity

_____
_____
_____
_____
_____
_____
_____

😋 FLAVOR WHEEL

Leather   Mushroom
Mineral   Woody
Earthy   Herbal
Honey   Spicy
Dark Fruit   Floral
Tropical Fruit   Grassy
Smoky   Coffee
Nutty   Chocolate

TASTE

☐ Sweet	☐ Tart	☐ Light
☐ Medium	☐ Fresh	☐ Medium
☐ Dry	☐ Flabby	☐ Full-Bodied

_____
_____
_____
_____
_____
_____
_____
_____
_____

💬 ADDITIONAL NOTES

_____
_____
_____
_____
_____
_____
_____
_____
_____
_____

FINISH

☐ Short ☐ Medium ☐ Long

_____
_____
_____

🍷 PAIRED WITH

☆ SCORE

/5☆

WINE Tasting

NAME	
VARIETAL	VINTAGE
PRODUCER	ALCOHOL %
REGION	PRICE
TASTED AT	DATE

👁 APPEARANCE

Color Hue
- ☐ Clear ☐ Pink ☐ Ruby
- ☐ Straw ☐ Salmon ☐ Garnet
- ☐ Gold ☐ Orange ☐ Purple
- ☐ Brown ☐ Brick ☐

Color Depth
- ☐ Pale
- ☐ Medium
- ☐ Deep

Clarity
- ☐ Clear
- ☐ Hazy
- ☐ Opaque

Viscosity
- ☐ Watery
- ☐ Medium
- ☐ Syrupy

AROMA

☐ Low ☐ Medium ☐ High Intensity

_____
_____
_____
_____
_____
_____

TASTE

☐ Sweet ☐ Tart ☐ Light
☐ Medium ☐ Fresh ☐ Medium
☐ Dry ☐ Flabby ☐ Full-Bodied

_____
_____
_____
_____
_____
_____
_____
_____
_____
_____

FINISH

☐ Short ☐ Medium ☐ Long

_____
_____
_____

😊 FLAVOR WHEEL

Leather Mushroom
Mineral Woody
Earthy Herbal
Honey Spicy
Dark Fruit Floral
Tropical Fruit Grassy
Smoky Coffee
Nutty Chocolate

💬 ADDITIONAL NOTES

_____
_____
_____
_____
_____
_____
_____
_____
_____
_____

🍽 PAIRED WITH

⭐ SCORE

/5 ☆

WINE Tasting

NAME	
VARIETAL	VINTAGE
PRODUCER	ALCOHOL %
REGION	PRICE
TASTED AT	DATE

👁 APPEARANCE

Color Hue
- ☐ Clear
- ☐ Straw
- ☐ Gold
- ☐ Brown
- ☐ Pink
- ☐ Salmon
- ☐ Orange
- ☐ Brick
- ☐ Ruby
- ☐ Garnet
- ☐ Purple
- ☐

Color Depth
- ☐ Pale
- ☐ Medium
- ☐ Deep

Clarity
- ☐ Clear
- ☐ Hazy
- ☐ Opaque

Viscosity
- ☐ Watery
- ☐ Medium
- ☐ Syrupy

AROMA
☐ Low ☐ Medium ☐ High Intensity

_____
_____
_____
_____
_____
_____
_____

TASTE
☐ Sweet ☐ Tart ☐ Light
☐ Medium ☐ Fresh ☐ Medium
☐ Dry ☐ Flabby ☐ Full-Bodied

_____
_____
_____
_____
_____
_____
_____
_____
_____
_____

FINISH
☐ Short ☐ Medium ☐ Long

_____
_____
_____
_____

😋 FLAVOR WHEEL

Leather Mushroom
Mineral Woody
Earthy Herbal
Honey Spicy
Dark Fruit Floral
Tropical Fruit Grassy
Smoky Coffee
Nutty Chocolate

💬 ADDITIONAL NOTES

_____
_____
_____
_____
_____
_____
_____
_____
_____
_____

🍷 PAIRED WITH

⭐ SCORE

/5☆

WINE Tasting

NAME	
VARIETAL	VINTAGE
PRODUCER	ALCOHOL %
REGION	PRICE
TASTED AT	DATE

👁 APPEARANCE

Color Hue
- ☐ Clear
- ☐ Straw
- ☐ Gold
- ☐ Brown
- ☐ Pink
- ☐ Salmon
- ☐ Orange
- ☐ Brick
- ☐ Ruby
- ☐ Garnet
- ☐ Purple
- ☐

Color Depth
- ☐ Pale
- ☐ Medium
- ☐ Deep

Clarity
- ☐ Clear
- ☐ Hazy
- ☐ Opaque

Viscosity
- ☐ Watery
- ☐ Medium
- ☐ Syrupy

AROMA

☐ Low ☐ Medium ☐ High Intensity

_____
_____
_____
_____
_____
_____
_____

TASTE

☐ Sweet ☐ Tart ☐ Light
☐ Medium ☐ Fresh ☐ Medium
☐ Dry ☐ Flabby ☐ Full-Bodied

_____
_____
_____
_____
_____
_____
_____
_____

FINISH

☐ Short ☐ Medium ☐ Long

_____
_____
_____

😋 FLAVOR WHEEL

Leather Mushroom
Mineral   Woody
Earthy   Herbal
Honey   Spicy
Dark
Fruit   Floral
Tropical
Fruit   Grassy
Smoky   Coffee
Nutty Chocolate

💬 ADDITIONAL NOTES

_____
_____
_____
_____
_____
_____
_____
_____
_____
_____
_____
_____

🍽 PAIRED WITH

☆ SCORE

/5 ☆

WINE Tasting

NAME	
VARIETAL	VINTAGE
PRODUCER	ALCOHOL %
REGION	PRICE
TASTED AT	DATE

⊙ APPEARANCE

Color Hue

☐ Clear   ☐ Pink   ☐ Ruby
☐ Straw   ☐ Salmon   ☐ Garnet
☐ Gold   ☐ Orange   ☐ Purple
☐ Brown   ☐ Brick   ☐

Color Depth

☐ Pale
☐ Medium
☐ Deep

Clarity

☐ Clear
☐ Hazy
☐ Opaque

Viscosity

☐ Watery
☐ Medium
☐ Syrupy

AROMA

☐ Low ☐ Medium ☐ High Intensity

_____
_____
_____
_____
_____
_____
_____
_____

TASTE

☐ Sweet   ☐ Tart   ☐ Light
☐ Medium   ☐ Fresh   ☐ Medium
☐ Dry   ☐ Flabby   ☐ Full-Bodied

_____
_____
_____
_____
_____
_____
_____
_____
_____

FINISH

☐ Short ☐ Medium ☐ Long

_____
_____
_____

☺ FLAVOR WHEEL

Leather   Mushroom
Mineral   Woody
Earthy   Herbal
Honey   Spicy
Dark Fruit   Floral
Tropical Fruit   Grassy
Smoky   Coffee
Nutty   Chocolate

☺ ADDITIONAL NOTES

_____
_____
_____
_____
_____
_____
_____
_____
_____
_____
_____

🍷 PAIRED WITH

☆ SCORE

/5 ☆

Printed in Great Britain
by Amazon

17395142R00063